ESC | European Studies Centre

Mutual Misunderstandings?

Muslims and Islam in the European media
Europe in the media of Muslim majority countries

Edited by Kerem Öktem and Reem Abou-El-Fadl

Contents

Preface   v
Sarmila Bose and Kalypso Nicolaidis

Acknowledgements   vii

Introduction   1
Mutual Misunderstandings - Muslims and the Media
Kerem Öktem

Chapter 1   France's conservative revolution and the making of an   13
             'imaginary Islam'
             Thomas Deltombe

Chapter 2   Images of the Middle East and Islam in German Media: 29
             A Reappraisal
             Kai Hafez

Chapter 3   Europe as a Media Myth: the Case of Bosnian Muslims   53
             Eldar Sarajlić

Chapter 4   Beyond Government Control: Divergent Views on Europe in   79
             the Egyptian Media
             Hanaa Ebeid

Chapter 5   Intimacy and contempt: the idea of Europe in the Turkish   107
             press
             Andrew Finkel

Chapter 6   Europe and Islam in Context, Identity *in* Politics: 127
             Concluding Remarks
             Reem Abou-El-Fadl

Selected Bibliography   145

Author Biographies   155

Preface

Thirty years after Ayatollah Khomeini's return to Tehran, twenty years after the Fatwa against Salman Rushdie, and seventeen years after the publication of Samuel Huntington's Clash of Civilisations, conflicts about Islam, Muslims and Europe have become a defining factor of identity politics on the continent. From the French disputes over the hijab to the 7/7 bombings of London, from the assault on Madrid's commuter network to the murder of Dutch filmmaker Theo van Gogh and the Danish Cartoon crisis, the last few years saw the unfolding of conflicts and acts of violence which exposed networks crisscrossing 'Muslim' suburbs, symbolic sites in city centres and seemingly distant locations in the Middle East. The media, ranging from newspapers and journals to television and the Internet, form a key arena in which such news is conveyed, and its impact amplified beyond all proportion, overburdened with narratives of threat and fear.

As the directors of two research centres at the University of Oxford, the European Studies Centre and the Reuters Institute for the Study of Journalism, we decided to collaborate to address this urgent topic. The European Studies Centre had been developing a major research project on the theme of 'Europe's Muslim Neighbourhoods: Minorities Within, Majorities Without', which investigates the impact of Muslim communities on Europe's relations with the Muslim world. The Reuters Institute had identified the representation of religion in media as a key area of research. Its thematic interest was not restricted to Islam alone; indeed it may be argued that it is impossible to assess the treatment of Islam in the media without a comparative perspective.

It was a stroke of luck, therefore, that the European Studies Centre and the Reuters Institute, having identified this common interest, received the opportunity to act on it thanks to a generous research grant from the Gerda Henkel Foundation. Together with the editor of this volume, Kerem Öktem, we convened a two-day workshop in May 2007 entitled 'Mutual Misunderstandings: Muslims and Islam in the European Media, Europe in the Media of Muslim Majority Countries'. There, we explored along with fifty participants, academics and journalists, the politics of identity construction and representations of Muslims in Europe, as well as the impact of Muslim communities on Europe's relations with the Muslim world. In addition to the authors of this volume, we were also fortunate to host Tariq Ramadan, Sarah Joseph, William Milam and Yunas Samad.

This volume contains five papers initially presented at the workshop and developed over the following year in an intensive intellectual dialogue between the authors and editors. They represent a wide array of different perspectives on representations of and conflicts about Islam, Muslims and Europe. The volume opens with a synopsis of the major research questions and results by Kerem Öktem, and concludes with a debate engaging conceptual insights from the literature on diasporas and post-colonial history by co-editor Reem Abou-El-Fadl.

We believe that this publication will help deepen our collective understanding of our 'mutual misunderstandings', whether between Muslims and non-Muslims in Europe, or between Muslim minorities, Muslim majorities, non-Muslim majorities or non-Muslim minorities, depending on the different settings where the debate is taking place, inside or outside Europe. We hope this book will help stimulate further intellectual curiosity to explore how religion, media and politics interact in today's ever more globalising world.

Sarmila Bose   Kalypso Nicolaidis
Director of the Reuters Institute   Director of the European Studies Centre
(2006 – 2008)   (2005 – 2009)

Acknowledgements

This collection of essays and the workshop on which it is based was made possible by the generous sponsorship of the Gerda Henkel Foundation, Dusseldorf, and the continued support of its Director Michael Hanssler.

Sophie Duchesne from the European Research Group at the Department of Politics and International Relations (DPIR) at the University of Oxford and the former director of the Maison Française d'Oxford, Alexis Tadié, helped to turn the initial workshop into a success.

My colleague Dimitar Bechev and the RAMSES Network for Excellence of Research on the Mediterranean, whose Oxford pillar he manages, made significant contributions in both financial and intellectual terms. Enver Ferhatovic introduced me to the Bosnian dimension of modern Muslim identities and thereby considerably expanded the scope of this volume.

The Reuters Institute for the Study of Journalism (RISJ) proved to be a congenial intellectual environment for hosting the initial workshop.

Neil MacFarlane, head of the Department of Politics and International Relations, David Levy, director of the Reuters Institute, and Timothy Garton Ash, Professor of European Studies and Honorary Chair of the European Studies Centre, commented on the draft manuscript, facilitated its editorial review and helped us greatly in bringing this project to its conclusion.

Julie Adams from the European Studies Centre and Esther Byrom from DPIR were the smooth operators who admirably managed the complex administrative logistics of this project.

Wasma Mansour (London College of Communication) dedicated dozens of hours of hard work to the very last-minute task of designing a truly striking cover page.

It was a great privilege to explore the pressing issues discussed in this volume together with my co-convenors Kalypso Nicolaidis and Sarmila Bose. Without the dedication and critical scrutiny of my co-editor Reem Abou-El-Fadl, this volume would have been a very different, and most probably much less engaging one.

Finally, my greatest thanks go to the participants of the workshop, particularly to Professor Yunas Samad from the University of Bradford, and to the contributors to this volume, who have succeeded in transcending the dichotomic readings of Islam vs. Europe, and who have provided us with an enlightened and insightful view of the multiple relations and dependencies encompassing Muslims, Islam, Europe and Europeans, as they are reflected in the media.

With its research project on *Europe's Muslim Neighbourhoods*, the European Studies Centre will build on this valuable work to explore further the interface of religion and politics in Europe.

Kerem Öktem

Oxford, March 2009

Introduction

Mutual misunderstandings?

Kerem Öktem

The current situation of Islam and Muslims in Europe has become one of the most controversial issues addressed in European public debates. Ever since the events of September 11th 2001, more often than not these debates have lacked empirical insight and have responded to perceptions of threats and fear. Substantial research, an in-depth knowledge of the communities under scrutiny, and a measured appraisal of their countries of origin, however, have often been absent from this discussion. Essentialising and Islamophobic arguments have become prevalent especially in continental European debates, often countered with self-victimising accounts of representatives acting on behalf of 'Muslims'. Not surprisingly, the central site of contestation over Islam and Muslims is the media, with its range of outlets including newspapers and magazines, television, radio and the much less researched 'new media' (Internet, blogs, online broadcasting).

This volume, and the Oxford workshop on *Muslims and Islam in the European media - Europe in the media of Muslim majority countries* on which it is based, seek to contribute to a more informed debate by shifting the geographic scope of inquiry. The volume looks from Europe to the Muslim world and from the Muslim world to Europe in five case studies – ranging from France and Germany to Bosnia Herzegovina, Turkey and Egypt. The choice of these countries reflects an intention to decentre the conventional focus on the Arab Middle East and Iran by adding cases from South East Europe such as Turkey and Bosnia, as well as by looking at Egypt, rather than at the more specific but over reported case of Saudi Arabia, as a trend-setting example in the Arabic-speaking Middle East. Throughout the case studies, and in the concluding remarks, we are led to question many assumptions which often tend to be taken for granted. These are the notions that there is a clearly delimited 'Europe', that this 'Europe' is opposed to a bounded 'Muslim world', and that conflict is written into the history and the present of the interaction between these two distinct 'worlds'. Hence, the attempt in this volume to unpack these highly aggregated, yet ultimately unhelpful categories.

Indeed, the authors of this volume, whether journalists or academics, establish that assumptions about a clear-cut Huntingtonian 'Clash of Civilisations' in the media and debates on 'Islam' and the 'West' are as unfounded as in other spaces of societal interaction involving Muslims and non-Muslims. The proposition that European media reporting presents a unified view on Islam and Muslims that is essentialising, reductionist and Islamophobic is untenable, given the diversity in different country contexts. So is the mirroring hypothesis that the media in Muslim majority or plurality countries follows an editorial line hostile to the West by default, lumping together the United States and Europe as one enemy. The case studies discussed in this volume establish that media debates in both sets of countries are highly differentiated, both internally, regarding target audiences, political positions, patterns of media ownership and access to information, and externally, above all regarding geographical proximity. In both cases, rather than being static and essential, images of the other change in response to political events and political debates.

In the EU, there appears to be a clear divergence between continental Europe and the UK. The media debate in Germany and France is more strongly influenced by perceptions of threat compared to the one in British media. The latter appear to be the most differentiated and best informed, at least in their quality outlets. Also, there seems to be no positive correlation between the experience of violence associated with Islam or Muslims in a country and the level of anti-Muslim sentiment or reporting and commentary driven by fear and resentment. Despite the absence of any such event in Germany, the debates there tend to accentuate Islam as an essential and negative marker of identity, probably influenced by the central role in the execution of the September 11th attacks of members of a cell based in Hamburg.

Where the three cases do share a common trajectory is in the historical evolution of the debates on Islam and Muslims. In all three countries, initially ethnic markers of identity (Turkish, Pakistani, Maghrebi) were superseded by the religious marker of Islam, even though the historical processes and ruptures after which immigrant communities had come to be named and treated as Muslims vary. In the Netherlands, it was Theo van Gogh's murder in 2004 and the debates around Ayaan Ali Hirshi. In the UK, as Yunas Samad suggested during the workshop, it was the Honeyford and Rushdie affairs in the mid to late 1980s, well before the London bombings of 7th July 2005, which attracted interest to Islam and Muslims as a threat. In Germany, the discovery of the Hamburg cell might have contributed to a feeling of entrapment and fear – even though neither the main Muslim community of the Turks, nor German-born Muslims were implicated in any way. The French debate really tipped over with the ascent to power of the Islamic Salvation Front in Algeria and the ensuing civil war in the 1990s.

The cases of Muslim majority/plurality countries discussed in this volume show that perceptions of Europe appear to be influenced less by essentialist judgements or even historical notions of Europe and rather by geographic proximity and levels of interaction and intimacy with EU countries. Secular and religious media in Pakistan – as suggested by William Milam during the workshop – tend to equate the West with the US, while Europe is at best seen as an appendix to the latter. Debates in the Mediterranean and South East

European countries, as represented in this volume, are far more differentiated, but also permeated by a romantic view of Europe as a trans-historical good. In Egypt, for instance, the European integration process is seen as a model for Arab unity. In Turkey and Bosnia, Europe is often referred to as a benchmark against which both the elites and the public measure their own political system, their level of economic development and cultural sophistication. At the same time, the omnipresence of EU institutions in the two countries – albeit in quite different forms - signals a deeper level of engagement, even if it is volatile and open to challenges from both nationalist and religious-conservative forces.

Finally, in addition to the structural conditions of media reporting on Islam, Muslims and Europe, imminent crises may trigger 'closures' of the debate. An example of a real divergence between countries with a large Muslim population and EU countries was the case of the Danish cartoon crisis, where opinion in the EU was divided, yet ostensibly unified from Bosnia to Pakistan, if differing in intensity and modes of expression. Unlike in the case of September 11th, July 7th or the Madrid bombings, where the range of opinions in the examined set of countries did not differ in substance from that of the EU countries, the cartoon debate seems to have accentuated divisions more clearly and facilitated a widely-shared 'Muslim solidarity'.

In addition to these empirical insights, this volume also suggests some methodological conclusions. Most of the studies presented are concerned with the debate in the print media and to a lesser extent in radio and television. While questions of media ownership and differentiations into tabloid and quality papers are important, so is a particular focus on the new media, including satellite TV and Internet. These outlets are much harder to assess in a scholarly fashion, yet they have become important parallel or counter-sites for the debate on Islam, Muslims and Europe.

The European, Muslim, and European-Muslim case studies

At the workshop, Yunas Samad drew attention to the changing representations of Pakistanis from Asian to Muslim in the context of wider debates on race and immigration in the United Kingdom. He examined the history of post-WWII immigration to the UK with a focus on the racial distinction between immigrants of Afro-Caribbean and Pakistani background. Debates prior to the 1980s constructed Afro-Caribbean communities as problematic and violent, while Asians were seen as docile, meek and law-abiding, with rather quaint if not antiquated cultural practices, yet closer to the white norm due to their perceived work ethic.

Unlike in continental European countries, Samad argued, multiculturalism has been established as a political norm in the UK since the 1990s, and legal provisions limit openly racist statements. This might explain why the debate shifted from race to culture, and religion emerged as a key marker of identity. The central turning points in the debate appear to be the Honeyford Affair in 1984 (on the education of Muslim children) and the fatwa by Ayatollah Khomeini in 1989 calling for Salman Rushdie's execution. Hence, by the time of September 11th and the London bombings, negative images of what by now had become a 'Muslim' community were widely available. Pakistanis, suggested Samad, were no longer seen as Asians, but as Muslims with too much of the wrong culture, living in segregated, violence-ridden communities. He argued that the media representation of Muslims now seamlessly blends images of terrorist bombers with the cultural critique of Islam as a religion of misogynist, hyper-masculinised young men.

Thomas Deltombe, in the opening chapter of the book, discusses the crises around Muslim identity in France by focusing on the mismatch of two factors: what he calls the 'elasticity' of Muslim communities versus the homogeneity of French identity. Tensions arise because Islam as a religious community does not possess a formalised clergy (elasticity), while French notions of citizenship and identity among elites, including journalists, are shaped by a sense of homogeneity. As a result, Islam is generally portrayed as a foreign immigrant religion, while it is reshaped in the image of Catholicism. Historicising this contention, Deltombe traces back the overlapping junctures to the first half of the 1980s, when Islam and Muslims emerged as a problem: the acknowledgement of the existence of Beurs (North African immigrants), the emergence of the Front National as a major political force, and the privatisation of television channels.

The point of rupture in France regarding the treatment of Islam and Muslims, therefore, appears not to have been September 11th, but events going back to the 1980s. After the Islamic Revolution in Iran in 1979, and the beginning of private TV broadcasts in the 1980s, argues Deltombe, the Rushdie affair in 1989 seems to have created a new set of conditions for the debate. The Algerian civil war in the mid-1990s finally led to the replacement of the term Beurs with the new term of 'Muslims' as indicator for North African origins. With the Algerian civil war, he suggests, a trend emerged in French public debate that tried to make sense of Islam through its most extreme manifestations, and in some instances equated Islam with a Fascism that had to be countered by a résistance. It was in this period that laïcité became the watchword for conservative elites and gradually turned into a 'pre-emptive weapon' against Islam and the headscarf. As the debate came to be dominated by conservative columnists, Islam and Muslim identity was increasingly presented as an issue of security. This conservative revolution has led to an 'imaginary' or 'imagined' Islam, concludes Deltombe, which is considered a potent threat to the values of the French Republic, while it excludes and stigmatises those who are invited to integrate as French citizens.

In his chapter, Kai Hafez examines the image of Islam in German mass media, by drawing attention to studies which only focus on the stereotypes of 'others', rather than looking at the full range of opinions and dissenting voices. He asserts that such studies run the risk of producing self-fulfilling prophecies. Suggesting that racist attitudes towards Islam have become less frequent in the German print-media, he concedes that the framing imagery of many articles dealing with Islam and Muslims tends to be de-contextualising and essentialising. In addition to visual essentialism, media texts are often characterised by a narrow focus on terrorism, violence and conflict, while issues of every-day life pertaining to Muslims are largely absent. In a comparable vein, eighty per cent of German TV features on Islam deal with questions of terrorism, violence in Muslim communities, domestic violence and the abuse of women. In light of this analysis, Hafez concludes that it is not so much individual texts that are Islamophobic but the composition of the media agenda, which is influenced by what he calls 'Enlightened Islamophobia'.

In his case study of Bosnia, an almost paradigmatically 'in-between' case, Eldar Sarajlić examines the relationship between ethnicity and religion, and the construction of Europe in the symbolic language of public debates. Bosnian Muslim identity is in many ways an outcome of the recent wars, when 'Muslimness' took on an ethnic content. While most newspapers, and most individuals in Bosnia are strongly in favour of secular life styles, Sarajlić contends, their very 'ethnic' identity is determined by their religious association as Muslim.

Europe is not a terra incognita in this sense, and the framework within which it is discursively constructed goes back further than the more recent emergence of Bosnian-Muslim (or Bosniak) ethnic identity. If the experience of Habsburg rule was a slightly more ambivalent one, including aspects of both colonial domination and modernisation, the dealings of Bosnian immigrants to Germany and Western Europe in the 1960s and 1970s contributed to the emergence of the notion of Europe as a benchmark of modernity. This affirmative view, argues Sarajlić, was further entrenched during the war, when Europe emerged as international mediator as well as the destination for tens of thousands of Bosnian refugees. The new myth of Europe as a 'trans-historical good' was built into the post-Dayton institutions of the nascent Bosnian state. 'Europe' was culturally defined as an ultimate and almost metaphysical 'political good' that all contemporary political movements strived to identify with. It is in this context that some of the crises of Islam in Europe were reflected by the Bosnian media. The Danish cartoon crisis did not lead to violence on the streets, yet was widely disapproved of. The criticism, however, was couched in terms of Europe's clash with its own values, and not depicted as an antagonism between religions or civilisations.

In her paper on Egyptian media debates on Europe and the West, Hanaa Ebeid distinguishes between political and cultural images of Europe. In parallel to Turkey, Egyptian newspapers often see themselves as the self-appointed guardians of the national interest, a self-image augmented by large levels of government ownership in the Egyptian media. Cairo newspapers are mostly government-owned, secular, pan-Arab nationalist and critical of America. In these media outlets, Europe is given considerable coverage only second to the United States and relations with other Arab countries, even though European matters are mostly confined to the news department. There is a relatively clear distinction between the European Union as a global player, and the Euro-Mediterranean Process, which involves Egypt more directly. The overarching image of Europe appears to be a romantic one, as it stands for European unity and the possibility of the fulfilment of the dream for Arab unity. In the realm of high politics and international relations, Ebeid argues, Europe is seen as a power broker in the Middle East and to a certain extent as a counter-hegemon counterbalancing US policy in the region. At the same time, though, the EU boycott of the democratically elected Hamas government tarnishes, in the eyes of the reading public, the image of Europe as a pro-reform actor.

In her discussion of Europe's cultural image, Ebeid highlights differences between the old and the 'new' media. While colonialism and religion were not normally evoked in the debate in newspapers and terrestrial TV stations, pan-Arab satellite channels like Al Jazeera have shifted the focus onto religious differences and introduced a more controversial tone of discussion. It is largely owing to the reporting of these satellite TV stations, she concludes, that the Danish Cartoon discussion for example was blown out of proportion and such large audiences mobilised. This conclusion also underscores her assertion that liberalisation in the media does not necessarily lead to more liberal content.

Andrew Finkel's account of the Turkish media scene concludes the case studies, and highlights Turkey's unique position as characterised by its intimate relationship with Europe, even though it is sometimes seen as its 'sick man'. Reminding the reader of the high levels of economic and political interaction between the EU and Turkey, with Turkey as the EU's seventh biggest trading partner in 2005, Finkel discusses the role of newspapers and television in the negotiation of sovereignty with the EU. Large parts of the mainstream secularist Turkish press act as self-proclaimed guardians of the nation and its borders, an outlook which the mass circulation newspaper *Hürriyet* declares daily with its motto 'Turkey belongs to the Turks' (*Türkiye Türklerindir*). Issues concerning Islam or Muslims in Europe are mostly read and discussed through the filter of a concern for Turkey's sovereignty and national integrity. In this way, even the argument 'Turkey is not admitted to the EU because it is Muslim' is recast as an issue of national sovereignty, not religion.

Globalising trends in the form of foreign media ownership, states Finkel, has so far had only a limited impact on Turkey, as most international networks have entered the country as part of Turkey-based joint ventures. International news channels like CNN Turk and the MSNBC-affiliated NTV, therefore, are both Turkey-based media outlets, which follow the same patterns of argument when it comes to questions of sovereignty and cooperation or integration with the European Union. One of the more remarkable aspects of the Turkish media debate on Europe, according to Finkel, is that the strongest pro-EU, and hence most pro-European editorial line is to be found in 'Islamist' newspapers such as *Zaman*, comparable in many ways to the Christian Science Monitor, i.e. a religious conservative editorial of high intellectual standing. While secularist newspapers cautiously guard the borders not only of the territory but also of the future of Turkey, the reporting of newspapers close to the governing party – at least until recently - suggests that the European project could even be integrated into the political discourse of the (Turkish) Islamist project.

Despite this emerging tableau of difference, however, there is also evidence for a general trend of deepening mistrust and misunderstanding between what may be defined in a reductionist manner as 'Muslims' and 'Europeans'. This could even be termed a 'closure of discourse'. The Danish cartoon crisis emerges as the most momentous rupture in this context, where very few observers managed to withstand the temptation to identify with one side or the other. On closer scrutiny, however, the case studies elucidate that each country has specific historical experiences of interaction, which have shaped the images of the other. For the media of distant Muslim-majority countries like Pakistan, Europe may be but a mere appendix of the US, which is perceived as the sole representative of the West. For debates in Egypt, Europe plays the dual role of a romantic model on the one hand and that of either counter-hegemon or lesser of two evils on the other. In Turkey and Bosnia, European intervention and interaction with European institutions and publics is at a much higher level, if divergent in substance. Here, Europe takes on the dual attributes of 'trans-historical' good and dominating 'other'.

As this volume shows, there is indeed a great deal of misunderstanding, yet not necessarily between two sides, but rather between different national, cultural and political actors – including the media - in the complex interplay of European politics, international relations and minority/diaspora debates. Indeed, members of European Muslim diasporas in western Europe have an important stake in this debate, and one which is often not heard, especially when it comes to the question of perceptions in Europe of Muslims and Islam. As Reem Abou-El-Fadl reminds us in her conclusion, the challenges they are facing today and the discussions they engage in might point us towards a more informed debate on Islam and Europe, and one that might be more accepting of both diversity and choice within and beyond Muslim communities.

Chapter One

France's conservative revolution and the making of an 'imaginary Islam'

Thomas Deltombe

Readers of French newspapers and audiences of French television channels are often told that 'Islam is going through a crisis', that there is 'a war between moderate and radical Islam', and that 'Islam is struggling to find its own place in Western society'. In short, we are constantly told that it is 'Islam' itself which is responsible for the scrutiny to which it has been subjected. This might be true in part. Yet this argument implies, firstly, that we all know and agree on what 'Islam' really is, and secondly, that public discourses faithfully reflect this 'reality'. This paper critically reconsiders these two presuppositions, to arrive at a very different conclusion.

In fact, the main reason why 'Islam' has become such a visible and hotly debated issue is to be found in the prejudiced manner in which public discourses and images are generated. In other words, I would argue that the 'Islam' which is presented by the media is not a reflection of 'reality' but rather the projection of opinion makers' fears and *imaginaires*, or even interests in something they have agreed to call 'Islam'.[1] For this reason, when it comes to representations, a distinction should be made between what Muslims individually consider to be their religion on the one hand – which is a difficult thing to grasp from the 'outside' – and what public discourses describe as 'Islam' on the other hand – which can be examined through the output of the French media.

---

[1]   As shown by Edward W. Said in *Orientalism* (New York: Pantheon Books, 1978) and *Covering Islam: how the media and the experts determine how we see the rest of the world* (London: Routledge and Kegan Paul, 1981).

This distinction might appear somewhat artificial, given that the way in which Muslims regard their own religion certainly influences the media, and that media discourses in turn change the way Muslims view their religion. However, the crucial point about this interaction is that it is not equal, and this inequality has arisen as a result of at least two factors.

First, the 'Islam' which is the most prevalent among Muslim communities in France is a religion without an identifiable clergy (comparable to the French Catholic hierarchical clergy, for example). Therefore, it is very difficult for French Muslims to agree upon a single, definite religious hierarchy and to project a centralised or uniform message of themselves as a religious community. In this context, external observers are left to choose the interpretations and representatives they deem relevant and satisfactory.[2] This remark is of prime importance in France, where Catholicism is the dominant religion, despite the state's claim to secularism. Convinced that 'Islam' is – or at least should be – as centralised as Catholicism, opinion makers fail to understand that, by selecting facts, spokespersons, words and images, they are inventing their own substitutes for this missing 'Muslim clergy'.

Second, this situation is reinforced by the fact that in France, 'Islam' continues to be seen as a minority religion with foreign roots. Considering themselves legitimate within the strict framework of democracy and national sovereignty, media and political leaders tend to disregard minority opinions: 'the majority rules'.[3] This silencing of the Muslim minorities is compounded by the remarkable homogeneity of the French elites. Originating from the same social backgrounds, educated in the same schools and living in the same neighbourhoods, the French political, media and economic elite remains very tightly-knit. For example, many prominent newscasters are married to high-

---

[2]   See also Olivier Roy, *L'Islam mondialisé* (Paris: Seuil, 2002).

[3]   Arnaud Mercier, *Le Journal télévisé* (Paris: Presses de Sciences-Po, 1996).

ranking politicians or prominent business people.[4] In this context, outsiders from lower socio-economic backgrounds and/or of foreign origin experience the greatest difficulties in having their voices heard.[5]

These two aspects – the elasticity of the concept of 'Islam' and the homogeneity of the French elite – have to be kept in mind in order to understand why and how 'Islam', or rather 'imaginary Islam', has been such a controversial issue in France for more than thirty years.

The re-emergence of 'imaginary Islam'

The public representation of 'Islam' in France went through a major rupture in the early 1980s, when the Iranian Revolution prompted a massive increase in interest in Islam within French media debates. Yet, besides this global event, 'national' events also contributed to the re-emergence of old images concerning 'Islam': these should not be discounted. Three are particularly important: the evolution of what until recently was called 'immigration'; the shift of the political spectrum towards the right; and the transformation of the French media industry.

By 1981, French television reported that the immigrant workers who had been 'imported' from the former French colonies were not leaving France, despite the dramatic increase of unemployment. Suddenly aware of this evolution, public attention turned to the children of these immigrants.[6] The media soon came up with a new label, 'beurs', to refer to French-born citizens of North African origin and, with this, came a crucial identity question. What is the criterion of full acceptance as a French citizen? And, still more

---

4 Serge Halimi, *Les nouveaux chiens de garde* (Paris: Liber-Raison d'agir, 1997).

5 Patrick Champagne, 'La vision médiatique', in Pierre Bourdieu ed., *La Misère du monde* (Paris: Seuil, 1993), and Patrick Champagne and Dominique Marchetti, *Censures visibles, censures invisibles* (Paris: Les Dossiers de l'audiovisuel, No. 106, INA, November 2002).

6 Edouard Mills-Affif, *Filmer les immigrés* (Brussels: De Boeck, 2004).

fundamentally, what does it really mean to 'be French'? To answer these questions, or maybe to avoid them, the question of the compatibility of 'Muslim' and 'French' identities – a question that had been abandoned since the end of the Algerian War in 1962 – returned to the front pages of news magazines and to the headlines of television news programmes.[7] An example comes from the cover of *Figaro Magazine* in October 1985, which showed a bust of Marianne (the Republican symbol par excellence) draped in an 'Islamic' headscarf: 'Will we still be French in thirty years?'[8] was the title.

The re-emergence of such images and mindsets is also a consequence of the evolution of the political spectrum. The 1980s saw the *Front National* become a major political force. A collection of Third Reich admirers and catholic traditionalists, nostalgic for French Algeria, the National Front managed to rally 10 to 15 per cent of the electorate on its nationalist platform.[9] Le Pen's movement thus posed a challenge for mainstream political forces: how could they attract Le Pen's constituency without appearing downright racist? While Le Pen was bluntly exploiting racist arguments and flattering white supremacists, traditional political forces soon discovered that 'Islam', coupled with the slippery concept of 'integration', could become a more subtle, and useful instrument.

Oddly enough, it was the Socialist Party, which first exploited the 'Islamic' argument to mask its ideological shift to neo-liberalism, two years after its 1981 accession to power. Confronted in 1983 with a massive workers' movement in the car industry – an economic sector employing many immigrant workers – the party leadership was determined to silence the strikers, who

---

[7]   Benjamin Stora, *La Gangrène et l'Oubli. La mémoire de la guerre d'Algérie* (Paris: La Découverte, 1991), and Yvan Gastaut, *L'immigration et l'opinion en France sous la Ve République* (Paris: Seuil, 2000).

[8]   *Figaro Magazine*, 25 October 1985.

[9]   See Edwy Plenel and Alain Rollat, *L'Effet Le Pen* (Paris: La Découverte - Le Monde, 1984).

ferociously opposed the Socialists' conversion to neo-liberal economic policy. President Mitterrand and several of his ministers described the strike as an event manipulated by 'fundamentalists, Muslims and Shi'a', following 'an agenda with little connection to French social realities'.[10] Derided by conservative critics of trade unions, the Socialist government now embarrassed their traditional supporters. *Nouvel Observateur*'s editor Jean Daniel, for example, denounced what he called 'the virtual transformation of every Muslim into an accomplice of Khomeini', and went on to ask: 'Shall we accept from a socialist government what we would not have tolerated from an opposition leader?'[11]

The Socialists' ideological U-turn soon made its impact on the left-wing media (starting with Jean Daniel himself), the third factor in the re-emergence of the 'Islamic imaginary'. The French press was undergoing a major crisis and felt the pressure to change. It was also in this period, roughly stretching from 1980 to 1985, that advertising started to become an economic necessity in the printed press. Even the left-wing daily *Libération* – founded by Jean-Paul Sartre in 1973 and widely known for its refusal to take on advertisements, as well as its criticism of the increasing influence of major corporations on the media – succumbed to the logic of the market. 'It is not *Libération* that has changed, it is advertising that has changed', its journalists now argued.[12] A greater revolution still occurred in the television sector.[13] At the same time as the Left was converting to an ideology of *laissez-faire*, a private television sector was emerging: the communication agency Havas launched *Canal +* (1984), media mogul Silvio Berlusconi purchased *La Cinq* (1986) and the

---

[10]   *Nord-Éclair*, 28 January 1983, Gilles Kepel, *Les banlieues de l'Islam. Naissance d'une religion en France* (Paris: Seuil, 1987).

[11]   *Le Nouvel Observateur*, 4 February 1983.

[12]   On the specific example of *Libération*, see Pierre Rimbert, *Libération de Sartre à Rothschild* (Paris: Liber-Raison d'agir, 2005).

[13]   Jacques Siracusa, *Le JT, machine à décrire. Sociologie du travail des reporters à la télévision* (Brussels: De Boeck, 2001).

company *Bouygues*, a leading construction conglomerate, entered the media market with the privatisation of France's largest television channel, TF1 in 1987. The private media sector soon became the driving force of the French media landscape.[14]

Unsurprisingly, with privatisation came an increasingly sensationalist treatment of news, where identity issues in general and 'Islam' in particular proved to be irresistible crowd pullers. As an example, we can cite an interview with the editor of the Catholic newspaper *La Croix*, conducted by Michèle Cotta, a prominent journalist working for TF1 and allegedly enjoying close ties to then President François Mitterrand: 'Don't you fear that a certain national identity may vanish because of our opening the doors [to immigrants]?', the journalist asked. She continued: 'More precisely and from a religious perspective, don't you fear that Catholicism, which is already enduring serious difficulties, will soon be surrounded by other religions, and will thus suffocate under their pressure?'[15] To illustrate this point, a report showing how 'Islam' had invaded a working-class neighbourhood in Northern France was broadcast.[16]

'Abstract universalism' vs. the 'Islamic veil'

As this example suggests, the ambiguity and elasticity of the term 'Islam' allows members of the cultural and political elite to express their nationalist anxiety through a socially and politically more 'acceptable' terminology that criticises Islam. While the National Front bluntly asserts the supremacy of white French Catholics, representatives of mainstream political forces feel uncomfortable with nationalist discourses so reminiscent of the darkest

---

[14] Jean-Noël Jeanneney ed., *L'Echo du siècle. Dictionnaire historique de la radio et de la télévision en France* (Paris: Hachette Littérature/Arte Editions, 2001).

[15] 'De bonne source', *TF1*, 11 February 1987.

[16] *Ibid.*

periods of French history. The fact that anti-Muslim rhetoric targets a *religion* constitutes a politically opportune alternative to racist discourses, especially in a Republic proud of its past battles against the intrusion of religion into the public sphere.

The conditions outlined above explain to a large extent how *laïcité* [laicisim], a central concept in the French Republican tradition, became the elite's watchword in the late 1980s. The re-emergence of *laïcité* in the public debate was further augmented in 1989 when the world was shaken by the Rushdie Affair, just as France was celebrating the bicentenary of the 1789 French Revolution. While media competition fuelled a sensationalist exploitation of the alleged 'Islamic problem', a problematic political consensus emerged. On the one hand, political leaders of the Left, who had given up some of their social ambitions a few years earlier, proudly re-emerged waving the flag of *laïcité*, a concept which they had long considered part of their very own political space. On the other hand, conservative politicians, traditionally reluctant to embrace a concept which had emerged to contain the influence of the Catholic clergy on French politics, agreed to join forces with their 'laïque' [secular] left-wing opponents when it became clear that 'Islam' was the sole target.

Hiding nationalist and ethnocentric sentiments behind religious images and humanitarian vocabularies, the crusade 'against the Islamic veil' and 'in favour of oppressed women' can be analysed as the elite's choice of an 'acceptable' version of, or response to, the National Front's racist ideology.[17] As sociologist Pierre Bourdieu put it as early as 1989, 'The explicit question – should we accept the so-called Islamic veil in state schools? – overshadows the implicit

---

[17] Said Bouamama, *L'Affaire du foulard Islamique. La production d'un racisme respectable* (Roubaix: Editions du Geai bleu, 2004).

question – should we accept immigrants of North-African origin in France?'[18] It is worth noting that Jean-Marie Le Pen, who had long been using Islamophobic discourse, abandoned this symbolic instrument to his mainstream competitors around that time. He would subsequently pride himself on progressing to what he called the 'real' issues, i.e. post-colonial immigration and national identity.

Thanks to the re-emergence of old *imaginaires* depicting 'Islam' as a brutal, irrational and dangerous phenomenon, the political and cultural elites of France became caught in an unprecedented conservative revolution.[19] Each time debates on the veil and *laïcité* resurfaced, throughout the 1990s and early 2000s, prominent left-wing intellectuals issued public apologies for their 'Marxist', 'relativist', and 'internationalist' commitments in the 1960s and 1970s, and accused those who remained faithful to their past activism of being irresponsible supporters of an outdated idealism.[20] Confronted with Khomeini's fanaticism, they argued, it is now time to face 'reality'. Echoing this new gospel, the former anti-colonialist journalist Jean Daniel, who had criticised the Socialists' Islamophobia during the 1983 automobile strike, promptly changed his mind and called the 'non-integration' of Muslims 'a crime against the French nation'.[21] At the same time, radical left-wing activist Regis Debray followed the same path and called for 'the defence of our civilisational genetic capital', embodied in the values of 'Enlightenment, Rationalism, the Republic and *Laïcité*'.[22] Islam, he suggested, had a different 'civilisational genetic capital'.

---

[18]   Pierre Bourdieu, 'Un problème peut en cacher un autre', in Charlotte Nordmann ed., *Le foulard islamique en questions* (Paris: Amsterdam, 2004).

[19]   Didier Eribon, *D'une révolution conservatrice, et ses effets sur la gauche française* (Paris: Editions Leo Scheer, 2007).

[20]   François Cusset, *La décennie. Le grand cauchemar des années 1980* (Paris: La Découverte, 2006).

[21]   This he proudly recalls in his recent book: Jean Daniel, *Cet étranger qui me ressemble* (Paris: Grasset, 2004).

[22]   'Océaniques', *FR3*, 4 April 1989.

The conservative turn in France is distinctive in that it wears the rhetorical mask of 'progress', 'modernity' and 'emancipation' – all concepts inherited from the 1789 Revolution and the Third Republic of the 1870s. During the 1989 'veil row', the editor of *Nouvel Observateur*, Jacques Julliard, professed the following: 'I believe that *laïcité*, a notion of Christian origin, represents decisive progress not only for Western Civilisations but also for Humanity as a whole'.[23] Editor of the conservative daily *Le Figaro*, Franz-Olivier Giesbert, echoed Julliard's enthusiasm for *laïcité* with a nostalgic reverence towards the assimilationist school system of the Republic, which compelled the colonised youth to embrace the mythical account of national history taught in the *métropole*: '*Laïque* and compulsory education gave generations of Blacks and Arabs Gallic ancestors. They even became perfect French people. This used to be the strength of Republic.'[24] It is indeed difficult to find any press article or television report dealing with 'Islam' that does not describe France, at least implicitly, as the 'homeland of Voltaire', the 'land of Human Rights', 'the country of Liberty, Equality and Fraternity', etc. This rhetorical strategy, of course, is nothing new: Napoleon made use of the generous principles of the French Revolution to justify his imperialist project, and the Third Republic mobilised universalist myths to conquer and maintain a vast colonial Empire. Why should the same principles not be used to legitimise the domestication – or 'assimilation' – of the 'Blacks and Arabs' living in 'our' suburbs?

The interlinked concepts of *laïcité* and 'integration' – the former apparently being the imperative condition of the latter – are the remnants of this ambiguous rhetoric. It hides exclusionary practices behind what political scientist Achille Mbembe calls 'abstract universalism'.[25] While 'integration'

---

[23] *Le Nouvel Observateur*, 26 October 1989.
[24] *Le Figaro*, 23 October 1989.
[25] Achille Mbembe, 'La République et l'impensé de la race', in Nicolas Bancel, Pascal Blanchard and Sandrine Lemaire, *La Fracture coloniale* (Paris: La Découverte, 2005).

could be understood as a social, political and economic concept that would concern all citizens, it has been emptied of these dimensions and transformed into a purely cultural instrument which mechanically excludes those who 'we' think do not share 'our' culture. *Laïcité* has had to endure a similar metamorphosis: initially, it offered a genuine mechanism for helping youth of whatever social, cultural or religious background to become French citizens. After fifteen years of massive media debate and political propaganda, it has deteriorated into a pre-emptive weapon which excludes those who are at first glance considered unfit or unworthy of becoming genuine citizens.[26] This is the real meaning of the 2004 law banning 'ostensible signs of religious belonging' (i.e. the 'Islamic veil') from state schools. Despite the recommendations of the Constitutional Council in 1989, what had remained a simple stigmatisation up to then became an institutionalised form of discrimination.

Security as an identity argument

Without the emergence of the discourse on 'Islamic terrorism', the evolution described above might never have succeeded. It would be fair to say that 'Islamic terrorism' is less the cause than the instrument of the French conservative revolution. What would have been treated strictly as a security matter otherwise, as used to be the case with other kinds of terrorist movements, is now regarded as an issue of culture and religion. Of course, Western politicians and journalists are not the only ones responsible for this situation, given that terrorists themselves couch their actions in religious rhetoric and employ (pseudo-)Islamic arguments. Yet the fact that the creators of public discourses rarely question the 'Islamic nature' of such phenomena, and that they generally accept and in fact reproduce the version provided by

---

[26]   Jean Baubérot, *Laïcité 1905-2005, entre passion et raison* (Paris: Seuil, 2004).

the terrorists themselves, suggests that they are not concerned with the pervasive confusion between security and identity issues.

Not only are French opinion makers comfortable with this problematic confusion, many of them in fact assume that there is a 'natural continuity' between the mere visibility of 'Islam' in the public sphere (as expressed in Islamic dress, the building of mosques, etc.) and the violent actions perpetrated by 'jihadists'. Former Minister of Interior, Charles Pasqua, clearly articulated this ideological position in 1997: 'The situation can be summed up with a few figures: in France, there are five million Muslims, one million who practice, 50,000 fundamentalists, and probably 2000 radicals.'[27] The hierarchy is quite clear: the more 'Muslim' you are, the more 'dangerous' you become.

Essentialising 'Islam' and regarding Muslims as a homogenous community in this way, many journalists and policy makers overlook the fact that Muslim communities are not only made up of individuals, but also differ from each other as groups. A telling example is a programme on the public channel France 2, a few weeks after the September 11th bombings, which introduced its guest, Soheib Bencheikh, as a 'religious Muslim' with a loyalty to the 'homeland of Human Rights'. Following coverage of the public execution of an adulterous woman in Afghanistan, the presenter turned to Bencheikh and asked: 'Are you able to feel the same way as we do when you see such images?' A few minutes later, when discussing 'Muslim radicals', the presenter addressed the 'moderate Muslim' once more: 'Do you promise, Mr Bencheikh (...) that your community will really help us get rid of [them]?'[28]

Thus mobilising an essentialist notion of Islam that turns every Muslim into a 'member of the community' accountable for the behaviour of the others, the discourse on 'Islamic terrorism' empowers those who wish to stigmatise and

---

[27] 'Sept sur Sept', *TF1*, 8 December 1996.
[28] 'Mots croisés', *France 2*, 8 October 2001.

discredit even the most discreet and uncontroversial expressions of 'Muslim' belonging. It is in this context that the emergence of 'Islamic terrorism' in the mid-1990s – with the Algerian civil war and the emergence of the Armed Islamic Groups (GIA) – created a welcome political opportunity for all kinds of Islamophobes.

Let us consider the arguments of Socialist Party leader Segolène Royal advocating the exclusion of veiled schoolgirls, aired on a television programme in 1994: 'Remember that there are killings in Algeria because of the veil! So let's not mix up all signs of religious belonging!'[29] Even though they are asked to differentiate 'Islamic', 'Catholic' or 'Jewish' signs of affiliation, consumers of the media are still constantly encouraged to see all expressions of 'Muslim' identity and all 'Islamic' phenomena as one homogenous challenge, be they normal or pathological, peaceful or violent, dangerous or welcoming.

What is striking in Segolène Royal's argument is that she – like many others – interprets 'Islam' through its most radical expression. She does not question the 'Islamic' nature of 'Islamic terrorism', nor consider other manifestations of this faith. The media play to their critical role by inviting what they call 'moderate Muslims' to talk shows. Still, it appears that these Muslims are carefully selected to embody, herald and legitimise the theories fashioned by the opinion makers. No wonder 'moderate Muslims' adamantly denounce – echoing the most reactionary politicians and intellectuals – what they call 'Islamism', which they frequently compare to fascism. In any case, this has the politically desirable side-effect of gaining them the prestigious title of 'Résistants' to Islamism.

The term 'Islamism', or Islamic fundamentalism, which has become all-pervasive in the French media treatment of Islam since the early 1990s, creates and maintains an artificial continuity between disparate phenomena.

---

[29]   'Journal de 20 Heures', *France 2*, 25 October 1994.

Presented as a solid 'reality', but never clearly defined, 'Islamism' is in fact an ideological tool for bundling security and identity issues together into a single category of 'threat'. This malleable and equivocal concept thus allows opinion makers to depict the wearing of an 'Islamic' veil as 'low intensity terrorism', the Islamic way of praying as an 'anti-Republican act of rebellion', or the refusal to eat pork or drink alcohol as 'suspicious practices'. We see here how 'zero tolerance' and 'pre-emptive war' models, formerly used against urban criminality in the United States, now penetrate the sphere of identity in France. Thus the most innocent sign of 'Islamic' belonging (identity) is regarded as a potential drift towards terrorism (security).[30]

Behind this logic, there is obviously the irrational fear of France's 'Islamisation', as illustrated by the *Figaro* Magazine's 1985 cover of the veiled Marianne. The debate on the *Jyllands Posten* cartoons of the Prophet Muhammad in 2006 provides one further example.[31] Those who refused to publish them were depicted as traitors to the nation by those journalists and politicians, who were in favour of publication of the cartoons. Why? Because, as a well-known 'left-wing' journalist explained, 'what the Islamists require is that we surrender ourselves'.[32] This argument was confirmed by a successful Algerian television journalist, presented as a 'moderate Muslim' by his French employers, who said: 'Those who rise up against the cartoons could, thanks to the same logic, forbid the Catholics from eating pork, the atheists from blaspheming or Western banks from using interest loans'.[33] These words are not a far cry from Le Pen's declaration in 1988, that 'If my ideas do not triumph, France is all washed up. The immigrants will be the kings and the

---

[30] Didier Bigo, 'Identifier, catégoriser et contrôler. Police et logique proactive', in Laurent Bonelli and Gilles Sainati, *La Machine à punir* (Paris: L'Esprit frappeur, 2004).

[31] Thomas Deltombe, 'Les médias français et les représentations du Prophète', contribution to the conference organised by the *Institut Français des Relations Internationales* (IFRI), 'Médias et construction des identités collectives en Méditerranée', Casablanca, November 2006.

[32] *Le Nouvel Observateur*, 9 February 2006.

[33] Mohamed Sifaoui, *L'Affaire des caricatures. Dessins et manipulations* (Paris: Privé, 2006), p. 165.

French Stock Exchange will quote in Arabic. In twenty-five years France will be an Islamic Republic'.[34]

Conclusion

More than thirty years after the accession of the Socialists to power and the emergence in the public sphere of citizens with origins in the former colonies of France, the French have become both the witnesses, and the victims of a dramatic conservative revolution. This process has been fuelled by a political, cultural and media elite eager to reassert itself in a changing society. Many Muslims legitimately consider themselves the prime target of this evolution, as it appears that 'imaginary Islam' has become a powerful instrument in the hands of an elite which has shifted the focus from genuine economic, social and political questions to a discriminatory focus on cultural and identity issues. The reactivation since the early 1980s of an 'imaginary Islam', which works as a mask for the ethnicisation of economic and social issues, has provided French elites with a powerful instrument that allowed them to justify their conservative ideological U-turn and shift the blame onto a stigmatised section of the French population. Although one can notice a similar evolution in other European countries, the instrumentalisation of 'Islam' in the French public debate is somewhat peculiar, as it finds its roots in a particular political structure as well as in a specific national history.

---

[34]   *Figaro Magazine*, 16 April 1988.

Chapter Two

Images of the Middle East and Islam in German Media: A Reappraisal

Kai Hafez

In 1981, three years after the publication of *Orientalism*, Edward Said wrote another work exploring Western perceptions of the Middle East and the Muslim world, called *Covering Islam. How the Media and the Experts Determine How We See the Rest of the World*. Once again, it demonstrated Said's impressive ability to dismantle the systematic misconceptions of the 'Orient'[1], stereotypical concepts of the Muslim 'Other', and the longevity of the Orient-Occident dichotomy in Western culture. This time, however, it was also somewhat prophetic, as it is fair to say that after the dissolution of the communist bloc, culturalist views of Islam began to fill the ideological vacuum that had opened up in Western societies. A milestone in this process was Samuel Huntington's paradigmatic thesis on the 'Clash of Civilisations', published in 1993. Its popularity revealed the striking ease with which an artificial mainstream perception of a dualism based on religion, or on a neighbouring 'race', can be constructed today that is quite similar to the thinking prevalent in the Middle Ages or in colonial times. The challenge this presents to the scholar, then, is to try to understand the communicative

---

[1] The 'Orient' is a concept that different authors have used for various regions of the world. In Said's work it is mostly confined to the Muslim world, or, even more precisely, to North Africa and the Middle East. In this text the same notion is applied, with the precision that the 'Middle East' includes Turkey, Arab countries, Israel, Pakistan, Afghanistan and Iran, and 'North Africa' contains the Arab countries and Mauritania and Djibouti. Both definitions are according to the systematisation of the German 'Institute for Middle East Studies' (Institut für Nahostforschung, former Deutsches Orient-Institut, Hamburg).

character of this hegemonic paternalist thinking in the mainstream media and public spheres of both the 'West'[2] and the 'Orient'.

Unfortunately, except for Said, few scholars have studied the constructive mechanism behind popular images of the Islam-West divide. Addressing this issue here, and taking Said's thesis as a departure point, the first observation to be made is that there is a certain structural similarity between Said and Huntington: both treated the 'Other' – 'Islam' from Huntington's perspective, and the 'West' from Said's – as some kind of cultural monolith. For Said, it was 'the media' and 'the West' that were simplifying a much more complex Middle East and calling it the hotbed of fanaticism and ignorance. It seems that Said himself failed to understand the very logic behind the construction of media discourses. On the one hand, Said's critique of the Western mass media's disparaging image of the Middle East and Islam is sound: after ten years of media research in the field of German, US and British media coverage of Islam and the Middle East, I am convinced that the mainstream media's image contains systematic defamation. On the other hand, media coverage in Europe is not made up only of stereotypes.

My critique of Said is based on the assumption that media texts produced for audiences in European and North American countries certainly do contain numerous stereotypes about the Middle East, but that there is much more to those texts than this. I argue that media content analysis should not be based merely on the socio-psychological concept of stereotypes or 'bias', because that method runs the risk of becoming self-referential. If one is searching for stereotypes, one will surely find them, but may not find the rest – the facts that are reported and the stories that are told – because of a basic analytical approach that is too limited in scope. Such an attitude allows an understanding of part of the media coverage, but not of the fabric of news, and how certain

---

[2]   Huntington confines the 'West' to Europe and North America.

events make it into the news while others do not. Nor is it then possible to understand the strange coexistence of high-quality journalism with what I would call the 'boulevardisation' of the Orient in the mainstream media of Europe and North America.

Moreover, text-centred media analysis based on concepts like stereotypes is merely speculative when it comes to the causes and effects of media coverage, because the news making process itself is not observed. Societies and cultures as a whole seem responsible for media coverage, while individual actors in the news making process such as journalists, news organisations, politicians, governments and consumers, as well as wider political cultures of course, remain obscure. The analysis of media texts without theoretical allusion to the news making process lends itself to conspiratorial thinking about the alleged influence of Western governments or Jewish lobbies and the like on Western media – an influence that can exist occasionally, but is surely not the whole story.

Systems theory of the media: the primacy of the national

To avoid such an analytical trap, I employ a theoretical framework inspired by different strands of systems theory. Here, media output is determined by a multitude of processes that are both autonomous and open to interaction with other sub-systems and social environments surrounding them.[3] Examples include the politico-economic system or the psychological system of the journalist, who is both a part of the media's professional role as well as his

---

[3]   For a more detailed outline of the theoretical approach in English see: Kai Hafez, 'The Middle East and Islam in Western Media: Towards a Comprehensive Theory of Foreign Reporting', in Kai Hafez ed., *Islam and the West in the Mass Media. Fragmented Images in a Globalizing World* (Cresskill, NJ: Hampton Press, 2000), pp. 27-66. The long version of my studies on foreign reporting and the Middle East in Germany has been published in German. The first volume is an elaboration of my theoretical approach, the second volume a documentation of my analysis of Middle East coverage of German national newspapers and weekly magazines (Kai Hafez, *Die politische Dimension der Auslandsberichts-erstattung*, Vol. 1: *Theoretische Grundlagen*, Vol. 2: *Das Nahost- und Islambild in der deutschen überregionalen Presse* (Baden-Baden: Nomos, 2002).

own environment. The national and international media are also important reference points for journalism. Finally, audiences are factors to be reckoned with, although they exert the most disparate influences, since only small parts, such as 'lobby groups', are organised, while most of the audience is dispersed and cannot be considered a single 'actor'.

In my view, the structural deficits in Western media coverage of the Middle East and the Muslim world are mostly based on the fact that even in today's seemingly globalised world, foreign reporting is, by and large, determined by national (and sometimes regional) interactions between the media system and other sub-systems and social environments. This pre-eminence of national over international interaction manifests itself in various ways. *Firstly*, there is a hegemony of national language communities creating their own long-term narratives of the world, and those discourses establish their own cultures and problems of intercultural understanding. *Secondly*, domestic political problems and issues often overlap with international issues or, worse, interfere with the way the world is interpreted and distort the original story. *Thirdly*, a primacy of national over international political influences can often be observed in wartime, when pluralist and very open coverage of conflicts in the Middle East and the Muslim world alternates with very narrow coverage that has the potential to reinforce international crises. *Fourthly*, since, in most cases, foreign reporting is predominantly directed at domestic audiences, national markets prevail over international markets and therefore foreign reporting often reproduces local concerns by selecting news that the local audience wants to hear and can understand. *Fifthly*, probably as a result of the insulation of markets, financial resources are often very scarce in foreign reporting: news agencies tend to be financially ill-equipped and newsrooms have little personnel, especially in the Middle East many Western media have to cover forty or so countries; low budgets in foreign reporting make the media susceptible to the public relations of governments and to propaganda. *Sixthly*, many journalists are badly educated and in most countries there are a very small number of Middle East and other area specialists in the main newsrooms of television, press and radio.

National media systems might be interconnected in the sense that foreign correspondents and news agencies in particular provide each national media system with the raw material of information. However, national media systems are not *interdependent*, since the way in which events are covered is not judged by those about whom the media systems report – in this case the people living in the Middle East and the Islamic world – but by domestic audiences. These people, due to their own distance from the matters reported, have hardly any means of judging the quality of the foreign news to which they are exposed. This is why domestic narratives, stereotypes, poor resources, bad education, and political interests are so often allowed to prevail over balanced information.

What at first seems to be a cultural problem is in fact an interaction between various national subsystems of the nation-state. These processes are almost universal, in the sense that language communities and nation states all over the world are communicative entities whose internal forces generate highly distinctive news output. This news has the potential to reinforce perceptions of conflict, which can easily lead to more tension in international relations. In specific environments, however, like in the contemporary European Union, national system dominance can start to give way to integrated regional structures and perceptions, as was perhaps the case during the British media coverage of the war in Iraq 2003 (see below).

If I hesitate to call these mechanisms of news making 'cultural stereotypes' or 'biases', it is because I consider the latter to be parts of the process: they do not completely determine the news content. The difference between other theoretical approaches and the one presented here is not simply a difference in terminology. It is far more significant, because viewing media coverage from the perspective of systems theory allows us to understand that national influences on news coverage are strong while global interdependence remains weak, although occasional learning processes in the media are possible. The dangers of a lack of interdependence in news making are tremendous. Nevertheless, the relative autonomy of national media systems in Western democracies does allow for occasional changes and flexibility in internal constellations. While problematic interactions between media systems and societal forces can lead to the distortion of media images, 'truthful' and 'neutral' information is also possible. *Firstly*, Western media systems are not so 'watertight' as not to allow any truthful facts on Middle East developments to enter the news. *Secondly*, at certain times, the dynamics of public controversy allow for Middle Eastern studies and other kinds of expertise to find their way into the mainstream media in order to clarify public misconceptions. *Thirdly*, a country's relative distance from involvement in a heated international crisis or even in war can liberalise public debates. *Fourthly*, overcoming the preoccupation of the public with certain domestic issues that interfere with foreign coverage, even though they have nothing to do with the Middle East, can also change perceptions.[4] *Fifthly*, stereotypes can be activated, but they can also be altered, depending on the kind of stereotype and how durable they are – some biases survive decades, others centuries or even millennia.[5]

To sum up, the images that Western mass media portray of the Middle East and Islam are often problematic, as Edward Said has rightly argued. Yet the 'image of the image' is very often also simplistic, because it underestimates

---

[4] See below, for instance, on the case of the German media debating the separation of the issues, 'Holocaust' and the 'Israel-Palestine conflict'.

[5] Franz W. Dröge, *Publizistik und Vorurteil* (Münster: Regensberg, 1967), p. 151.

cultural dynamics and those of the media system. It is only if we look at the real character of media content and production processes that an opening up of Western systems towards the Middle East and Islam can be imagined in the future.

The image of the Middle East and Islam in the German Press

Having introduced the arguments and preferred method of this investigation, this section presents the empirical results, based on a large study conducted on the image of the Middle East and the Islamic world in the German press. Around 14,000 articles were coded, analysed and interpreted using both quantitative and qualitative methods. While it is not possible to extrapolate too much from these German results, they do constitute a valid case study for a Western media system covering Islam.

Quantitative Results

Before taking a closer look at media narratives, we first examine some quantitative data on what kind of topics and facts were presented over the last few decades in the German press. These results allow a first glimpse into the strengths and weaknesses of news reporting.

Extent of Coverage: increasing, but still rudimentary

One positive result is that, compared to other regions, coverage of the Middle East has grown continuously in German media, and the region receives more attention than other world regions, such as Africa or Latin America (Hafez 2002a, Vol. 2, pp. 43 ff.). This increase in coverage started in the 1970s, and today, news and reporting on the Middle East have reached about the same level as those on North America. What makes these results less impressive is the fact that, on average over recent decades, not more than three articles a day on the Middle East have been published in national papers – a number that must be compared with the mass of articles that are published about the Middle East in the region's own newspapers. The 'density of imagination' in Germany, as I would call it, is still rudimentary.

Moreover, this growth in news output was largely spurred by an increase in coverage of major world events, such as the Six Day War, the oil crisis of 1973, the Iranian revolution and the Gulf wars. Coverage of these events was sometimes very extensive, but coverage of the region itself frequently ebbed away with the end of events, which points to a low degree of continuity in news production. It is often much easier to report on aspects of a certain war or other sorts of political violence than it is to report about the subsequent peace negotiations or other signs of normalisation, as these constitute less dramatic news to German papers.

In addition, during the 1970s, a gap grew up between the increasing amount of newspaper coverage of the Middle East and the almost stagnating number of reports in political magazines. This can be seen as a sign that the German media, allowed for a steady growth in event-centred newspaper coverage, without providing the same amount of contextual information necessary to understand or analyse it.

In the final analysis, the Middle East and North Africa are regions about which the Western consumer receives much less information than about his/her own country and region, and rather a growing amount of poorly contextualised and often discontinuous pieces of information. Since it seems that more news about the Middle East cannot be digested by audiences, due to the constraints of everyday life, this is not to argue for more news. In fact, as will become clear later on, certain aspects of politics in the Middle East are almost over-reported. Instead, what is needed is more *contextualised* news and information.

Subject Areas: news routines and politically oriented views of the Middle East

About four-fifths of German newspaper and magazine reports over the last thirty years have dealt with political issues. Economic information counts for below ten per cent, and other subject areas like culture, entertainment, tourism and religion (in the narrow sense of religious teachings and practices) make up no more than about two per cent of coverage. Given that the mass media play an important role in shaping international perceptions, the German press has thus paved the way for a politically centred view of North Africa, the Middle East and the Muslim world. The normality of everyday life escapes this media perspective.

It is interesting to note that religion hardly plays a role in such coverage – only 'political Islam' features. This is also true for Judaism, of which we hear almost nothing except for its Zionist connotations.[6] This has interesting implications for other news coverage. For example, the Judeo-Christian heritage of Europe and the Occident is a term frequently used in the debate on Turkish accession to the European Union. Yet it is arguably little more than a slogan, based on the legacy of the Old Testament at best, because contemporary Judaism is not very prominent in German mass media feuilletons. Similarly, contemporary Middle Eastern culture is almost invisible.

Another of the project's observations was that entertainment subjects, such as stories on the Persian Shah Mohammed Reza Pahlevi, on King Farouk or Aga Khan, for example, that were prominent front page news in the German and Western mass media in the 1950s and early 1960s, had vanished completely by the end of the 1960s. This development coincided almost exactly with the Six Day War of 1967, irrespective of the fact that figures like the Shah of Iran

---

[6] Hafez, *Die politische Dimension*, 2002, Vol. 2, pp. 114 ff. In contrast to my findings, Detlef Thofern argues in his single-medium study on the German weekly news magazine *Der Spiegel* that the religious substance of Judaism gets more attention than that of Islam. Detlef Thofern, *Darstellungen des Islams in DER SPIEGEL. Eine inhaltsanalytische Untersuchung über Themen und Bilder der Berichterstattung von 1950 bis 1989* (Hamburg: Lit 1998), p. 77.

continued to rule and other monarchs kept on living their extravagant lives in exile. Therefore I would argue that the war was actually the first of a series of political shock waves that went through Western media, politicising the news and changing the whole system of news making. The second shock was the Iranian revolution and the rise of Islamic fundamentalism.

Yet we should not forget such observations about the post-war period: after the Second World War, entertainment and cultural aspects of the Middle East did make front page news in the West. While one could argue that the absence of Middle Eastern cultural and religious reporting seems to support Edward Said's position with regard to the cultural stereotyping of the Middle East by a Western media system like the German, this study's findings raise a major methodological objection: a missing agenda is no proof for the essentialist profiling of the 'Other'. The real problem is not so much what journalists and the public *think of* the Middle East, but what they *think about*, which is the classical agenda-setting paradigm in communication science. Large parts of the Middle Eastern and Muslim realities are just not reported in the German media. News gets rejected before it is even given a chance to be stereotyped. Moreover, the relatively short-term changes in news media culture with regard to entertainment issues show that there might not be a long-term, 'Orientalist', culturally *imbibed* bias at work in the selection of topics. Perhaps in the future we will be able to find ways of reviving older media cultures of diversity or develop new forms of cultural and entertainment approaches to the Middle East and North Africa.

If 'culturalism' is, as I argue, a poor explanation for such changes in media cultures, a far more plausible answer might be that great events tend to create their own news standards. Scholars found out a long time ago that news values guide the process of the selection of news.[7] For instance, news about 'violent' and 'nationally relevant' events are usually valued highly. Judgments on what qualifies a certain event as 'relevant', to stay with the example, can be routinised in a particular news room or other discursive spheres such as the German media system.

In the case of the coverage by German national papers of the Middle East and North Africa, there was a step-by-step worsening of standards, and the creation of news routines to which all players – news agencies, journalists and audiences – adhered. Of course, this seems unreasonable, because despite all the problems in the Middle East, there are enough positive events to report about (for example, an improvement in university education standards in most countries during recent decades), and there are enough reasons to treat the Middle East not *only* as a politically dangerous 'Near East'. While it is notoriously difficult to forecast tomorrow's media images, the documented shift in German coverage of the Middle East *and* North Africa that took place in the 1960s has shown that changes are possible. Thus future positive events that challenge existing news routines and revise existing news values – for example a viable democratic reform movement in the Middle East – could well diversify German media perceptions.[8] It is not that German mass media do not react to the realities on the ground. They rather oversimplify. Learning processes in modern mass media seem much slower than one would expect, based on their otherwise fast, often real-time news coverage.

---

[7] Johan Galtung and Mari Holmboe Ruge, 'The Structure of Foreign News', *Journal of Peace Research*, Vol. 2, No. 1, pp. 64-91; Winifried Schulz, *Die Konstruktion von Realität in den Nachrichtenmedien* (Freiburg: Alber, 1976).

[8] An example of this is the improved image of politics in modern Turkey that has been conveyed since democracy was revived in the 1990s. See Hafez, *Die politische Dimension*, 2002, Vol. 2, pp. 134ff.

Negativity as a news value

The media's focus on political issues makes diversification of the news agenda necessary for another reason: it almost inevitably leads to another problem, a conflict-centred view of the Middle East and the Muslim world that has the potential to increase tensions in international relations. Having analysed this large sample of German press coverage over a period from the 1950s to the 1990s, I found that one third to one half of the core events covered in the articles (depending on the kind of newspaper or magazine) were violent events such as terrorism, wars and assassination.[9] Since this is a long-term average, it happens that at certain times, often lasting weeks and months, the absolute majority of news from the Middle East has been about political violence. This creates the image of a chaotic Middle East. Although media effects on people's opinions are hard to gauge using scientific means, it seems plausible that the concentration on negative news creates the widespread feeling in German society that the Middle East is a dangerous place – an area of the world where you had better not go.

A correlation of data showed that, not surprisingly, political news contains much more violence than, for example, cultural news. Therefore the strong focus on political news in Middle East coverage creates an image of a remote part of the world that appears in sharp contrast to the consumer's image of his or her local or national world. The latter contains conflicts, and sometimes violence, but also many other aspects such as entertainment and culture. We do not need comparative studies to show that there is currently more political violence in the Middle East than in Western democracies. Yet despite this, the social reality on the ground is often not as fierce and brutal as it seems through the 'binoculars' of German mass media. The reason many Westerners have prejudices against the Middle East might be deep-rooted cultural

---

[9]   See *ibid.*, pp. 59ff., 90f., 92ff., 125ff.

stereotypes, but they are also exposed to an often dehumanising image of life in the Middle East that contains politics, violence and not much else.

The high level of negativity in political reporting is not only a result of the nature of Middle Eastern politics, since even partly liberalised autocracies in the Arab world feature regular political behaviour and political debate, as well as elections. When Western media report these events, they tend to prefer highly institutionalised forms of regular politics, namely elections, referenda or changes in leadership (such as the succession after the death of King Fahd in Saudi Arabia). We only occasionally hear about ongoing political debates, and civil societies such as those in today's Egypt or Morocco, where governments are so often criticised and their policies debated in the national press. Meanwhile, when German news about the Middle East goes through the bottleneck of limited resources (usually publishing two to three articles a day), they tend to select news about violence. The situation is not much better when other parts of the world are covered. South American revolutions and African wars are all big news. The causes of such news standards can only be inferred, and not really proven empirically, because solid newsroom studies are rare and difficult to conduct. Some communication scholars argue that in the eyes of many consumers and journalists, the main function of the news media is to act as a warning system for dangers or potential dangers that develop in the outside world. Comparative research in various media systems of the world has shown that such news standards are a universal feature. Political violence in Ireland and Spain, or Islamist terrorism for example, make for preferred news. Still, there is also a certain North-South gap in the sense that political developments in the United States and Europe often receive more attention in non-Western media, because the US and Europe are at the centre of the global system.

Topics of Negativity: political Islam and Israel/Palestine

Continuing with the analysis, our findings about negativity can be correlated with single topics *within the subject area of political news*. We find that there are enormous differences that make it necessary to alter the assumption that the German media hold a consistently negative image of the Middle East. I shall demonstrate this by comparing two long established news topics on the German news agenda: political Islam and the Israeli-Palestinian conflict.

While in 20 to 40 per cent of all news items, violent events were the reason for German press reports on the Israeli-Palestinian conflict, this was the case in 40 to 70 per cent of all reports where 'Islam' was the major topic. There are obviously very different standards of reporting in various topical fields. 'Islam' is the single most negatively connoted topic in Middle East reporting in Germany. The reason for this can be deduced by looking at the chronology of news about Islam over the last four decades. It shows that prior to the Iranian Revolution in 1978-9, 'Islam' was hardly part of German news. Starting with the revolution, however, and inspired by a number of conflicts and international scandals such as the Rushdie affair, and, of course, the September 11th attacks, 'political Islam' became the object of public interest, rather than Islam as a religious or cultural phenomenon.

Underlying this are two completely different perspectives on conflict in the German media. Political Islam has been increasingly seen as an equivalent to terrorism rather than a political-cultural movement that has existed for over half a century and includes various aspects from actual opposition to existing authoritarian regimes, from social activism, to political violence of various kinds. Meanwhile, the Israel-Palestine conflict is seen as a 'civilised' conflict that can be solved. In other words, while political Islam is basically seen as a criminal phenomenon, the Israel-Palestine conflict is perceived as a substantial political problem with many different aspects, from violence to diplomacy to

41

regular political behaviour. This reductionism seems to conflict with Khalid Duran's argument that the really important phenomenon in many Muslim countries is the broad socio-cultural streaming of neoconservative 'Re-Islamisation' rather than Islamic fundamentalism, which is a much smaller phenomenon but receives most attention in Europe and the US.[10] Moreover, most German media outlets have had difficulties in understanding the difference between moderate and extremist strands within fundamentalist political movements.

In fact, some Western governments have cooperated with certain 'fundamentalists' as diplomatic partners – consider EU-Iranian relations or relations between the US and Algerian, Egyptian or Turkish Islamists.[11] Yet that dialogue has not entered the media to any significant degree. The media have not learned that there is an imbalance between political culture and media culture in the West in the sense that the media are consistently stigmatizing political Islam as opposition movements, Western governments are pragmatically cooperating with those forces.

It seems that as long as Islamism is involved, a more balanced news agenda may not be achieved. In recent years, after German media were criticised for Islamophobia, many journalists began to pay lip service to the fact that Islam is not identical with fundamentalism. Yet they have continued to report news of fundamentalism or jihadism, with very few stories about aspects of moderate Islam.[12] With regard to this narrow view of 'Islam' – not of the whole Middle East – Edward Said and others who have said that there is indeed a deeply engrained cultural bias in the West that resists learning processes seem to be justified. The social psychologist Dröge differentiated between long-term

---

[10] Khalid Duran, *Re-Islamisierung und Entwicklungspolitik* (Munich et al.: Weltforum Verlag, 1982).

[11] See Fawaz Gerges, *America and Political Islam: Clash of Cultures or Clash of Interests* (Cambridge: Cambridge University Press, 1999).

[12] On the various branches of reformist Islam see, for instance: Mehran Kamrava, ed., *The New Voices of Islam. Reforming Politics and Modernity: A Reader* (London et al.: I.B. Tauris, 2006).

cultural, mid-term epochal and short-term contemporary stereotypes. It seems to me that Islam is a long-term stereotype. While the Israeli-Palestinian conflict has been ongoing for sixty years and the image of Palestinians has improved or deteriorated several times (see below), the negative image of Islam in Western mainstream literature and culture is over 1000 years old. Since the Crusades and the time of Christian reformation and throughout colonialism, negative images prevailed over marginalised positive ones.[13]

Islam is not only a single, isolated topic, but a sub-theme that can appear in all other subject areas and topics, in politics as much as in culture and the economy. If it is true, as I would suggest, that there is a Western cultural bias against Islam, it seems to be comprehensive.

Countries of Negativity: the news geography

Moving from the topics of negative images to the geographical focus of such coverage, we can safely assert that the German media's images of the Middle East and North Africa are far from being homogeneous. An analysis of which Middle Eastern countries receive attention allows us to discern a specific news geography or news mapping. First, there are a limited number of 'white spots' in German news, because countries like Yemen or Oman are hardly ever covered. More importantly, there is a clear focus on the news of the Mashreq countries (Palestine, Jordan, Iraq, Lebanon and Syria) and of Egypt, while news of the Maghreb, Sudan, the Arabian Peninsula, or countries like Pakistan and Afghanistan are much rarer. Since this is the average result of a long-term analysis from the 1950s to the 1990s, some might argue that certain things could have changed after the September 11th attacks, which was considered by many a turning point in the West's relations with the Middle East. However, after the initial attention paid to Afghanistan and Pakistan in 2001 and 2002,

---

[13] See Zachary Lockman, *Contending Visions of the Middle East. The History and Politics of Orientalism* (Cambridge: Cambridge University Press, 2004).

the prominence of those countries in German media seems strongly confined to the Western 'war on terror' in the area and could certainly end thereafter.

The news geography of the Middle East in the European media certainly differs from country to country. In France, for example, there is more awareness of the Maghreb. However, the fact remains that the image of the 'Orient' is not a unified phenomenon: it comprises various zones of attention and imagination. We simply have much more information available in our media systems about those parts of the Middle East and North Africa that offer prior 'news values' to us. News value is defined, for example, by international conflicts in the Middle East or cultural-historical proximity to certain countries, for example Egypt in the case of Germany and England, or Algeria and Lebanon in the case of France.

Interestingly, there is no correlation between the volume of bilateral trade and the volume of news coverage. While Germany conducts about half of its foreign trade in North Africa and the Middle East with countries like Turkey, Iran and Pakistan, these countries are the subject of only about 20 per cent of media reports.[14] It is a combination of political interests, international relevance of conflicts and cultural proximity that determines foreign reporting, and not so much economic interest or socio-demographic factors such as the size of a country's population (see also Unland 1986). Even today's large coverage of Dubai is to a large driven by cultural fascination of a booming modernity and new opportunities for tourism (the mega-hotels and the like), and less by economic considerations. In-depth reporting about the fact that the harbour of Dubai is ten times bigger than Germany's largest port Hamburg and that the people of Dubai might very well revitalise their traditional trading culture at the crossroads of the Middle East is a side-show to German media.

---

[14]   Hafez, *Die politische Dimension*, 2002, Vol. 2, pp. 65 ff.

Regardless of the news values, a correlation of the country ranking with topical analysis shows that the more a country is represented in the German news, the more balanced the composition of subjects areas is, and the greater the chance of it escaping extreme concentration on political issues. If we further correlate these results with the analysis of negativity, we find there are basically three types of countries in the German news geography. There are blank spots like Yemen, which rarely surface in newspapers and media outlets. Then there are countries that are covered often because of political violence, but also because of non-exceptional political events like elections or issues of succession in government. This applies to many Gulf states, Israel, Egypt, or Turkey. Finally, there are countries whose image is very much confined to violent conflict, i.e. Lebanon, Iraq, Iran, Syria, Afghanistan, and Sudan.

Thus what sometimes seems like a stereotypical monolith – German reporting about the Middle East and North Africa – is in fact a complex news geography. It consists of various spheres of density of reporting and awareness, and of more or less 'moderate', balanced and differentiated patterns of perception of political developments.

Qualitative Results: Framing, Discourse and Narratives

What remains to be explored is the qualitative aspect: how news stories are told, and what kind of frames and narratives are used. Since this is a vast field, and since it escapes quantitative content analysis, it is hard to give a representative answer. Instead, I would like to elaborate on a few case studies that show how interaction processes between media narratives, the media system and the national 'environments' of the media can be interpreted. In other words, how can the politico-economic complex and various segments of the audience and the public interfere with the media image of Islam and the Middle East and North Africa? I will concentrate on cases of international conflict in the Middle East, crises of various types such as the oil crisis of 1973 (an economic, non-violent crisis), the Israeli-Palestinian conflict (a long-term conflict with various phases and aspects of both violent and diplomatic activity), and recent wars in Afghanistan (2001) and Iraq (2003). A crisis is by definition a turning point within a conflict that can lead to increased tension and violence, to stagnation or to resolution and settlement.

Before we try to interpret the cases, a few words about the framing of those events are in order. The first case is that of the coverage of the 1973 oil crisis in the German press, which went through roughly three phases.[15] The initial phase, when the conflict began, was characterised by different approaches in the German press: this ranged from leftist-liberal sympathy with the Arab countries' endeavours to narrow the North-South gap in international relations, to conservative interpretations of the events as a danger to German national security and welfare. At the peak of events, after the October War of 1973, the coverage changed and the leftist-liberal segment of German newspapers took over the national security and welfare frame of the conservative papers. For about two weeks, while the OPEC boycotted the US and the Netherlands, it was almost as if there was full consensus in the German press that the Arabs had no right to do what they were doing. After the crisis was over, however, the coverage changed again and the liberal magazine *Der Spiegel*, to mention but one example, launched a whole series of articles on the exploitation of Arab countries by American and British major oil companies.

The next case is the German coverage of the Israeli-Palestinian conflict. I conducted a full-text analysis of the major newspapers during major events such as the Six Day War, the October War, the negotiation of the Camp David

---

[15] Hafez, *Die politische Dimension*, 2002, Vol. 2, pp. 180 ff.

Accords and the Lebanon invasion of 1982.[16] On the whole, there was a tremendous change in overall framing. While in 1967, Germany sided almost completely with Israel, the media since changed step by step, applying a much more balanced approach that accepts both Israel's right of self defence and the national aspirations of the Palestinians, albeit with variations among newspapers mostly depending on the political spectrum to which they belong.

The third example is the wars in Afghanistan 2001 and Iraq 2003.[17] In Germany, the question of whether or not the Afghan war was justified was not even debated, nor ever high on the agenda. This changed dramatically before, during and after the Iraq War of 2003. While in the United States, almost all mainstream media supported President Bush during the war, or at least did not allow for significant criticism, Germany's media were much more pluralist in their approach, allowing for anti-war, as well as pro-war voices to express themselves in articles, talk shows, etc. While 80 per cent of Germans, as well as the government, were against the war, opinions in the media were diverse. The situation seemed comparable to that in countries like Spain with the difference that the Aznar government was pro-war, but the Spanish people were against it, and the Spanish media systems comprised various elements from pro-government television to critical newspapers.

On the basis of all three, my interpretation of the framing and storytelling points in different directions. In countries that experience existential crises or else engage in full-scale war, the mass media seem ready to 'rally around their flags', supporting their governments, and what they define as their 'interests': a behaviour that has been recognised in modern media studies.[18] For short periods, the media's ability to act in a pluralist way and attach weight to Middle Eastern perspectives can be seriously curtailed. This is what German

---

[16] Hafez, *Die politische Dimension*, pp. 144 ff.
[17] Hafez, 'Die irrationale Fehlwahrnehmung', 2002; Hafez, 2004.
[18] See John E. Mueller, *War, Presidents, and Public Opinion* (New York: Wiley, 1973).

philosopher Hannah Arendt observed during the Vietnam War and what she labelled the 'mentality of raison d'état' – a serious threat to the plurality of Western democracies (Arendt, 1967, 1971). The case of Spain – a country that was involved in Iraq but which maintained diversity in the media – does not disprove this rule, because Spanish military engagement was on a limited scale, and did not activate the 'flag rallying syndrome'. The British example seems more interesting: I conducted a small content analysis of several British newspapers' coverage of the war and was impressed by the relative diversity maintained even in wartime (Hafez 2004). Although there were patriotic trends, this was certainly a much more 'distanced' coverage than, for instance, that during the Falklands War.

There are a number of reasons for the media to 'rally around the flag' when a country is engaged in war or feels threatened. *Firstly*, Western governments have learned to walk a tightrope between information and disinformation. Well-known examples include the US government's campaign on Iraqi 'weapons of mass destruction', and the British government's publications.[19] *Secondly*, the media system itself is highly vulnerable to government propaganda, because one-sided government information 'trickles down' through news agencies into newsrooms.[20] The growing speed of news production makes checks on information almost impossible. *Thirdly*, mainstream audiences are often ready to rally around their flags, and there are always some powerful organised sectors in the public sphere, namely lobbyists, who support this trend.

While the mass media gain autonomy, manoeuvrability and diversity at regular intervals by playing politicians and audiences off against each other, this system collapses at wartime, because both groups push the mainstream media

---

[19]   See Howard Tumber and Jerry Palmer, *Media at War. The Iraq Crisis* (London: Sage, 2004).
[20]   Hafez, 2007, pp. 24 ff.

in the same direction, making them active co-combatants of their governments.

The British case of 2003 is somewhat mystifying, but one might argue that British media coverage was exhibiting signs of a slow and gradual Europeanisation. In other words, due to the process of integration into the European Union, the national media system has perhaps been losing its dominance and opening up to trans-border influences from other European countries, *despite* the Euro-scepticism within the country. However, this is mere speculation and we have no empirical evidence to support it.

Apart from cases of war, German media are capable of retaining a critical distance. While media reporting during crises is a real problem, Western conflict reporting is on the whole much better. This is visible in the coverage of the Israeli-Palestinian conflict.[21] Their coverage shows that if countries like Germany do not have to rally around their flag, or if the conflict as such is of a long-term nature, as in the case of the Israeli-Palestinian conflict, the potential of German media to uphold diverse images of Middle Eastern conflicts increases.

Firstly, political lobbies and interest groups can be influential for a short time, but they are only one factor influencing media systems, and they do not control the media. *Secondly*, in times of conflict de-escalation, right and left wing political cleavages within the media allow for more diversity in their approaches (for example, the question of Turkey's accession to the EU is firmly entrenched in such party orientations, and these are echoed in German media). *Thirdly*, apart from times of high-intensity warfare, often meaning tight media control by the military, the visibility of human tragedies can activate the core humanist values of a society (note the first Intifada of 1987, which improved international attitudes towards the Palestinians). *Fourthly*, in

---

[21]   Hafez, *Die politische Dimension*, 2002, Vol. 2.

long-term conflicts such as the one between Israelis and Palestinians, domestic political cultures can undergo changes that can be conducive to changes in foreign reporting – for instance, German coverage of the conflicts was long overshadowed by the memory of the Holocaust and it is only very slowly that these issues are becoming dissociated from one another.

Conclusion

On the whole, under certain conditions, German foreign reporting on the Middle East can be firmly entrenched in nationalist argumentations that ridicule all talk of globalisation and of global exchanges in media systems. At other times, however, coverage is very diverse – a diversity Edward Said and many other critics of the Western media's coverage of the Middle East and Islam have probably not given enough credit. While many quantitative data, for example the strong focus of the German national press on violent issues related to Islam, seem to support Edward Said's argument of a stereotypical 'Orientalist' negative view of the Middle East and North Africa, we must admit that selectivity in news is no full-fledged stereotype. A constant media focus on issues like terrorism *implies* stereotyping on the side of the audience, but it is no *explicit* denigration of the 'Other" as inferior or evil. Moreover, a closer look at the complexities and changes of relevant discourses and narratives demonstrates that we must be careful not to overstate homogenous media coverage in Western Europe. What is needed are state-of-the-art analyses of media texts, narratives and a reflection on the multiple causes and effects of Western views of the Middle East and the rest of the Muslim world.

Chapter Three

Europe as a Media Myth:
The Case of Bosnian Muslims

Eldar Sarajlić

Europe is crippled by everything that simplifies it by idealization, abstraction and reduction. Europe is a *complex* [...] distinctive in its ability to bring together differences [...] and inseparably connect the opposites.

Edgar Morin, 1987

As contemporary anthropology tells us, communities are symbolically constructed subjects[1]. Every group of people that considers itself a part of a particular community *imagines* this communion through a number of available symbols, deployed in a public discourse. Being inherently social, a person is a symbolic animal, as Ernst Cassirer has put it.[2] Hence, the order of the world, or the way we understand it to be, is not a thing by itself: it does not exist independently of our perceiving structure, but is rather embedded deeply in our language. We can thus say that the world – both in the broadest and the narrowest sense of the word – exists primarily in the domain of language and discourse, from where it affects our social and political affairs. According to Cassirer, '...the special symbolic forms are not imitations, but *organs* of reality, since it is solely by their agency that anything real becomes an object

---

[1] Anthony P. Cohen, *The Symbolic Construction of Community* (London: Tavistock, 1985).
[2] Ernst Cassirer, *Language and Myth* (New York and London: Harper & Bros, 1946).

for intellectual apprehension, and as such is made visible to us'.[3] Recalling the words of Wittgenstein, today we say that it is language that 'contains reality', not the other way round.

In this paper, I focus on the question of discourse and how the use of a particular notion of 'Europe' in media discourse has contributed to the construction of an exclusive and reductive *ethno-religious* identity in the Bosnian context. I claim that, unlike other countries in the Middle East with large Muslim populations, Bosnian Muslims regard 'Europe' as a positive power and utilise its symbolism in building their identity. I focus on media narratives and draw my conclusions from their political and social utilisation, believing that any particular discourse both reflects and *constitutes* relations of power, and that it is this constitution that must be subjected to scientific and critical scrutiny.

This conjecture implies that if one can say that the contemporary notion of 'Islam' – as an aggregation – is a vague term without clear social, cultural or political meaning, then the same can be said for the notion of 'Europe'. This is all the more evident when these two terms – 'Europe' and 'Islam' – are juxtaposed and as such employed in a dialectical discourse, influenced by power, ideology and everyday politics. However, when employed in a discourse that does not make dialectic exclusions, but produces a complementary and coherent value-system, 'Europe' and 'Islam' create a particularly interesting symbolic setup, strongly intertwined with the politics of identity, power and political legitimacy.

As I intend to show, this is exactly what happens in Bosnia and Herzegovina today, where the Muslim community participates in a symbolic interplay between notions of 'Europe' and 'Islam'. Thus I will speak about 'Europe' as a

---

[3]   *Ibid.*

phenomenon constituted by media discourse, and I shall refer to the Bosnian Muslim (*Bosniak*[4]) *ethno-religious* identity as the final destination of these narrative processes. The hypothesis of this paper is that the notion of 'Europe' – as it is being conceptualised through the media discourse in Bosnia and Herzegovina – is a form of political myth. It is used to ensure the legitimacy of the collective cultural claims of Bosnian Muslims *as an ethnic community* based on primordial notions, and thus to further reduce the sphere of the polity to exclusive cultural elements.

'Europe' as a Political Myth: Narrative of the Ultimate Good

Firstly, I wish to clarify what I consider to be the contemporary *political mythology of Europe,* a phenomenon peculiar to societies on the margins of the European Union. There are clear theoretical foundations for the interpretation of this phenomenon in the social sciences. The political myth, as explained by French sociologist Raoul Girardet, represents some sort of a 'displaced superstructure', a skewed or subjective, unreliable, disputed explanation of reality.[5] Yet as a particular narrative, it has – without doubt – some explanatory value: it offers a key for understanding the present. Myths order the 'confusing amount of facts and events' around us by making use of an archive of symbols and emotional ties understandable to many, often drawn from the pool of religious sentiment or tradition. But, political myths are almost never born out of mere respect or observance of tradition. They are always linked to concrete historical and political reality, or as Girardet clearly

---

4   It is difficult to make a clear distinction between the *Bosniak* and the *Bosnian Muslim,* since these two terms overlap in meaning: they both essentially describe the political (as national) identity of Muslims living in Bosnia and Herzegovina. However, since the aim of this paper is to argue that the *political* dimension of this identity is being pushed aside in favour of exclusively religious and cultural (thus *antipolitical* in my understanding) dimensions, the term *Bosniak* will be used less frequently than *Bosnian Muslim.*

5   Raoul Girardet, *Politički mitovi i mitologije,* XX Vek, Beograd, 2000 [*Mythes et Mythologies Politiques,* Paris: Seuil, 1986], p. 13.

indicated, to a particular social turmoil or a trauma.[6] It is a fact that societies undergoing transition are more likely to be affected by mythological discourse. By this I mean not only the national-messianic mythology that has obviously gained momentum in many transitional societies, but a specific, latent yet influential mythology related to the construction of 'Europe' as a powerful social and political symbol. I consider the region of Southeast Europe to be paradigmatic in this sense: even before the 'confusing facts and events'[7] related to transition of this region started to multiply, some elements had already made the region more sensitive towards the adoption of a simplistic, ideological myth narrative related to the meaning of 'Europe' as an *ultimate good*.

Speaking geopolitically, one can even say that socialist Yugoslavia – once it dissolved into ethnic states – was somehow geopolitically predetermined to fully internalise a narrative that speaks of 'Europe' as a domain of higher ontological reality. There are two principal reasons for such a claim. First, the country's post-Second World War existence was, to a large extent, marked by a differentiated political balance between the Socialist and Western bloc. The West itself (especially after 1948) – as an embryo of what Europe means today – was not considered as radically different. Unlike the case of other socialist countries of Eastern Europe, in Yugoslavia, the West was not perceived in terms of an ideological enemy, but rather as an ideal model for the growing mass culture. Historical facts, with regards to trade, cultural exchange or travel, clearly show this different conception of Europe in Yugoslavia, not as a 'class enemy' but rather as a symbol of affluence and economic prosperity. Unlike their neighbours in Eastern Europe, a great number of Yugoslav workers (many of whom were Muslims from Bosnia and Herzegovina) saw Western

---

[6] *Ibid.*, pp. 57; 92; 206; 211.
[7] *Ibid.*

Europe not as a *Terra Incognita,* but as a desired complex of economically progressive societies.[8]

Secondly, after Yugoslavia's collapse, these notions have remained in the popular understanding in most countries of the region, including Bosnia and Herzegovina. This is due to the specific role of European countries in the conflict, both as political mediators and as destinations for thousands of refugees. The mixture of this epistemic background and the 'confusing amount of fact and events' after the war broke out in 1992 led to a specific symbolic construction of Europe where the values – as desirable models – of peace, democracy, the nation-state, progress and prosperity started to dominate public opinion. Yugoslavia's location at the edge of Europe, along with the evident failure of its successor states in the transition process, and the conflict that was generated by their autocratic regimes, has further supported the popular understanding of Europe as a social and political ideal. To an ordinary Balkan citizen in the nineties, Europe was, as Croatian writer Slavenka Drakulić put it, '...something distant, something to be attained, to be deserved. It is also something expensive and fine: good clothes, the certain look and smell of its people. Europe is plenitude: food, cars, light, everything – a kind of festival of colours, diversity, opulence, beauty. It offers choice, from shampoo to political parties. It represents freedom of expression. It is a

---

[8] Like many of their peers in the West and in Yugoslavia, between 1960 and 1990, the Muslims of Bosnia and Herzegovina saw wearing jeans, listening to the Beatles and Rolling Stones, watching MTV after it appeared and drinking Coca-Cola as 'European behaviour' and as supreme signs of 'modernity'. Popular western culture even penetrated the sphere of tradition: in rural areas, young Muslim girls began wearing tight jeans for example, enraging their parents and village elders. In doing so, they sought to liberate themselves from the traditional matrix of behaviour and to join 'Western modernity', which seemed more attractive than their own traditions. See for example Tone Bringa, *Being Muslim the Bosnian Way: Identity and Community in a Central Bosnian Village* (Princeton University Press, 1995).

promised land, New Utopia, a lollipop. And through television, that Europe is right there, in your apartment, often in colours much too bright to be real.'[9]

As this passage shows, there is a particular understanding of 'Europe' in Balkan transitional countries, generated by a particular historical and geopolitical setting that had shaped the mass consciousness and created a specific phenomenon. I shall refer to this phenomenon as the *Media Myth of Europe*. It represents a symbolic language phenomenon that emerged from the dynamics of the relationship between the media and politics. It is constituted by uncritical representations of newly emerging post-socialist political categories used by the media system, in which the notion of 'Europe' played a key role for identification and categorisation. What makes the Media Myth of Europe different from a mere 'discourse' is its obvious reference to a higher ontological reality in which 'Europe' is understood as some sort of metaphysical saviour that is to relieve the society from a dreadful transitional hardship.

In Bosnia and Herzegovina, this was also enabled by the lack of substantive knowledge about the new political categories that had penetrated the public domain after the collapse of communism. Without any serious academic involvement, and instead with journalists and politicians constructing the notion of 'Europe' in the public sphere, the phenomenon encompassed both discursive (based on words) but also symbolic (based on pictures) horizons of the public domain.[10] The mythological narrative of 'Europe' has even been

---

[9]   Slavenka Drakulić,*Café Europa: Life After Communism* (Penguin, 1996), pp. 11–12.

[10] A confirmation of the vivid words of Slavenka Drakulić, and of the idea that the notion of 'Europe' is being infused with certain divine characteristics, comes from Bosnia and Herzegovina, where 'Europe' is frequently being associated with metaphors of light. For example, an editorial on citizens' travel visa issues in the daily paper *Oslobođenje*, entitled 'The Lights of Europe', contained the following: '[h]appy days are ahead of the citizens of Bosnia and Herzegovina... If everything goes as planned, our sports players, cultural workers and members of the religious communities will have an opportunity to see the lights of the European cities. Unfortunately, the aforementioned groups represent only a small portion of the population of Bosnia and

built – in quite a banal way – into the foundations of the state of Bosnia and Herzegovina. A brief look at the official flag – with its blue and yellow background covered with a line of five-pointing stars indicating the 'European' character of the state – reveals this fact.

At this point, a specific distinction can be made between two complementary patterns of understanding and communicating 'Europe' in the public sphere of transitional countries. On the one hand, as a symbol, 'Europe' is used as a mythological instrument for explaining complex reality and identifying dominant values. On the other hand, as a narrative practice, the Media Myth of Europe is predominantly used for processes of 'othering'.[11] These create and emphasise an identity boundary, as well as generating legitimacy for given policies and projects, by public appropriation of the symbolism of 'Europe'.

As a symbol of the ultimate good, 'Europe' is ubiquitous in Bosnia and Herzegovina. It can be found across the public sphere, from state heraldry to commercial marketing campaigns in which certain products will be marketed as boasting 'European quality' or essence. This kind of setup makes 'othering' through appropriation of European symbolism an easily commenced practice and a pattern wielded across the public sphere.

To a large extent, this pattern is akin to the ways mythologies function. Mythological discourse in politics, as an ideology, is dialectical. There are two sides of any value order, so the analysis of such discourse must reflect both poles, in order to come up with a critical conclusion. In the contemporary case

---

Herzegovina; the others will, as in the past, be forced to dwell at the entrances of embassies and consular offices, applying endlessly for an entrance visa, which nobody can guarantee they will be provided with. [There is] Not even an explanation if they get refused...' *Oslobodenje*, 7 June 2006. This is particularly interesting bearing in mind the frequent usage of the metaphor of 'light' in any mythological or religious discourse. See Girardet, *Mythes*, p. 13.

[11]   See an interesting discussion in Alain Brossat, 'Europe: Us and Others' in *European Identity of Kosova*, International Symposium, Forum 2015 Pristina, 2008, pp. 25-31. Available online at: http://www.forumi2015.org/home/images/stories/identity.pdf

of the Media Myth of Europe in Bosnia and Herzegovina, it is the 'Balkans' that serve as the opposite pole. Drawing on Said's *Orientalism* (1979) and Todorova's *Imagining the Balkans* (1997), mainstream social science explains that this symbolic axis ('European' versus 'Balkan') primarily reflects communitarian struggles of identification and categorisation. As a consequence of its identifying character and categorical power, 'Europe' has become a sort of floating object, a powerful symbolic mechanism that can be employed in different (sometimes even in totally opposite) political contexts. As for example, Manchester anthropologist Stef Jansen has shown, in the Balkans, 'Europe' as a positive qualification was equally employed by both nationalist and anti-nationalist forces. The nationalists aimed to present their ethnic identity as genuinely 'European', and therefore civilised and superior to the 'Balkan' one. This was a feature of Croatian and Serbian rightist discourse in the nineties. Meanwhile, some anti-nationalists (in Croatia, Serbia and Bosnia and Herzegovina) wanted to distance themselves from what they saw as 'non-European' ethnic and national ideology and employed a similar discourse identifying themselves with 'Europe' and 'European' values. The point at which this discourse converged with the 'Orientalist' one – the work of Milica Bakić-Hayden (1995) is relevant here[12] – was the evident identification of 'Europe' with an array of 'desired social virtues and individual characteristics',

---

[12] It seems that the category of 'Europe' in this case stems from the Orientalist dichotomies Bakic-Hayden describes in *Nesting Orientalisms*. Here, the pattern of reproduction of the original dichotomy creates a new reality and allows for the symbolic motion of subjects along the ideological axis. In such a pattern, Bakic-Hayden argues, 'Asia is more "East" or "other" than eastern Europe; within eastern Europe itself, this gradation is reproduced with the Balkans perceived as most 'eastern'; within the Balkans there are similarly constructed hierarchies.' Milica Bakic-Hayden, 'Nesting Orientalisms: The case of Former Yugoslavia', *Slavic Review* Vol. 54, No. 4, Winter 1995, pp. 917-931.

which resulted in Europe being 'displaced from its planetary location and introduced into the world of metaphors'.[13]

Based on this, we can conclude that most of the actors calling upon 'European values' in today's Bosnia and Herzegovina practice identifying and categorising acts aimed at legitimising and promoting a certain political outlook. In other words, they employ expressions of power to identify and categorise, aiming to reconstitute the existing identities and legitimise the given social and political order in the new global setting. As such, 'Europe' does not represent a practical term with determined semantic boundaries, but rather varies in relation to the subject employing it, acquiring a completely relative meaning that depends not only upon the situation, but upon the *intention* of the communicative subject.[14] It becomes a functional and manipulative tool, shaped and tailored to create and legitimise the subjects of political power.

Europe and Bosnian Muslims: From Colony to European Identity

There are hardly any major differences in popular understandings of 'Europe' among different ethno-religious groups in Bosnia and Herzegovina, despite the claims of their different historical experience with European countries during the nineteenth and twentieth centuries. Indeed, as confirmed by various

---

[13] Stef Jansen, 'Svakodnevni orijentalizam: doživljaj „Balkana" / „Evrope" u Beogradu i Zagrebu', Filozofija i društvo, br. 18, 33-72, Beograd; ['Everyday orientalism: the experience of 'Balkan'/ 'Europe' in Belgrade and Zagreb'], p. 49.

[14] Kimberly Coles makes a similar interpretation in the article 'Ambivalent Builders: Europeanization, the Production of Difference and Internationals in Bosnia and Herzegovina': 'Europe... is an increasingly "dominant symbol" ... in the 20th Century... an icon that embraces a whole spectrum of different referents and meanings... It is by no means a stable object.' Kimberly Coles, 'Ambivalent Builders: Europeanization, the Production of Difference and Internationals in Bosnia and Herzegovina' in X. Bougarel, E. Helms, G. Duijzings, *The New Bosnian Mosaic: Identities, Memories and Moral Claims in a Post-War Society*. (London: Ashgate, 2007), p. 261.

polls,[15] Muslims in Bosnia and Herzegovina hold more or less the same opinions on the qualities and character of 'Europe' as members of other religious groups in the country. Nevertheless, there is also some historical specificity that deserves to be analysed in more detail.

The first collective experience of the Bosnian Muslim population with Europe was one of colonialism: the Habsburg Empire that had occupied Bosnia and Herzegovina in 1878 produced the first substantive reactions to European identity, both from the feudal elite and the overall populace. This took the form of resistance to the modernisation of identity symbols: the intellectual discussion about the type of hat a Muslim in Bosnia was allowed to wear is an interesting example.[16] Despite the apparent banality of the issue, it was understood as a crucial and existential matter where modern (as 'European') and traditional (as 'Muslim') identities collided in a way that was to determine the fate of Bosnian Muslims. Clearly, Muslim identity was considered to be threatened by various modern social trends, as a result of occupation by a European power.

On the other hand, the subsequent industrialisation and transformation of a once exclusively agricultural society softened this collective feeling. Thus attitudes towards Europe started to change, although a large portion of the older and mostly rural population remained suspicious of everything related to Europe. The viability of the modernist stream of Muslim thought was further strengthened by certain intellectuals sponsored by the Habsburgs, who supported the process of what was labelled as 'the Europeanisation'[17] of

---

[15]   Survey conducted in July 2005 by the Delegation of the European Commission in Bosnia and Herzegovina, which showed that Europe was predominantly identified with economic prosperity by all constituent ethnic groups in the country.

[16]   Enes Karić, 'Bosanske muslimanske rasprave za i protiv obnove i reforme u XX stoljeću', in Bosanske muslimanske rasprave, Hrestomatija I, Sarajevo [Bosnian-Muslim Discourses on the Reform in the Twentieth Century], 2003, p. 9.

[17]   Ibid., p. 9.

Bosnian Muslims. Their activities were interpreted as an attempt to create a 'European Islam' in Bosnia and Herzegovina.

Although there was also a significant part of the intellectual community that had tried to advocate a third way that would have gone beyond this black and white division, the dialectic of *traditional vs. modern* identification predominated Muslim-Europe relations during the late nineteenth and much of the twentieth century, when the balance started tipping in favour of the modern. To a large extent, this was also due to a transposition of classes within the Bosnian Muslim community that had come to the fore in the first half of the twentieth century. With the coming of socialism, understood as modernity's apogee in the Balkans, for the first time in its history, the Bosnian Muslim working class took over the political prerogatives that had belonged to the elite members of Ottoman society. However, this was not an *ex nihilo* event. It had been preceded by a gradual process in which the social and political status of the community's elite had significantly deteriorated.

The incorporation of Bosnian Muslims into European types of empires and states – first by the Habsburg monarchy and the subsequent state/kingdom of Yugoslavia, and then by socialist Yugoslavia – has had a profound influence on Bosnian Muslim identity. In this time-span, from 1878 to 1945, the community has gone through difficult phases in which its social status was fundamentally changed. A former privileged social group during the Ottoman rule, characterised by a strong and influential feudal elite, became a second-classed community in the Habsburg Empire and the subsequent Kingdom of Yugoslavia. The feudal elite was stripped of most of its economic privileges and positioned much lower on the social ladder, opening the way for the working class to take the lead in representing the entire community. The trend continued until the Second World War, when the majority of the Bosnian Muslim working class joined the ranks of the antifascist resistance taking part in the creation of a socialist state of Yugoslavia. On a historical scale, this transposition coincided with modernity's most important impact on the Bosnian Muslim community: its first ever political recognition within the framework of modern statehood. However small and at moments hardly recognisable (especially until 1974 when the political status was constitutionally confirmed), this recognition occurred in a distinctively *modern* and *European* ideological setting. Ideological categories employed elsewhere in Europe were wielded to justify and legitimise the establishment of Bosnian Muslims as an ethno-national community with full political attributes.[18]

The fact that modern values came to dominate the ways in which Bosnian Muslims as a community see themselves today reveals not only the prevalent attraction of modernity for identity construction. In this particular case it also clearly shows the contingent character of any identity relationship in which the identities at stake depend upon current political interests much more than upon some particular cultural or historical 'essence'. To Bosnian Muslims, modernity also brought new means to craft their identity, use tradition and modern politics to come up with their own national narrative, and build themselves as a distinct ethno-national community. In this narrative, the notion of 'Europe' plays one of the most important roles.

The reasons why such modern ideology has constructed 'Europe' in this way are quite simple: as a symbolic entity, Europe has been very useful for the social and political categorisation necessary in every ethnicity's construction process, and the Bosnian Muslims have realised this fact. This is not to underestimate the power of the complex historical experience of the European

---

[18] The Marxist and especially Leninist political philosophy, in which notions not only of class but of *national* liberty also had a significant ideological importance, has been successfully employed in this context, contributing to the establishment of Bosnian Muslims as a distinct ethno-*national* community. See an interesting overview presented in Kasim Suljević, *Nacionalnost Muslimana* ('The Nationality of Muslims') (Rijeka: Otokar Keršovani, 1981).

presence in Bosnia and Herzegovina and the popular response to it – there are many facts confirming its utmost relevance.[19] However, the phenomenon reaches far beyond facts of history, regardless of whether they represent evidence in favour of, or against the 'Europeanisation' of Bosnian Muslims. Instead, the focus must be directed towards the existing media discourse, as a key point where modernity exerts its symbolic power.

Media, Muslims and 'Europe'

The character of the media sphere in Bosnia and Herzegovina is complex. First, the media situation itself reflects the complexities of the country's modern existence – the transition from communist to democratic environment, the war and subsequent reconciliation process, and, most importantly, the ethnic divisions that are still pervasive in all walks of life. Secondly, the number of media sources in Bosnia and Herzegovina, if compared to the size of the country's population (around four million) is relatively high, with up to 190 radio and television stations, six daily papers and forty weekly magazines.[20] Except for several exclusively religious media sources,[21] most media are secularly oriented and do not employ an explicit religious label. Due to the clear prominence of the 'secular' over the 'religious' media – in terms of press

---

[19] One historical example confirming the previous notion is the existence of the institution of the Grand Mufti (*Reis-ul-Ulema*) as the *direct* consequence of Habsburg (as 'European') presence in Bosnia. This institution became central to the identity of Bosnian Muslims – Bosniaks – as such. See Fikret Karčić, *Bošnjaci i izazovi modernosti, kasni osmanlijski i habsburški period,* (Sarajevo: El-Kalem, 2004).

[20] Cf. OSCE Report, *The State of Media Freedom in Bosnia and Herzegovina: the Public Service Broadcasting,* published on 29 March 2007. More information is available at http://www.osce.org/documents/rfm/2007/03/23751_en.pdf.

[21] Here I refer specifically to the Muslim religious periodicals – *Preporod, SAFF, Novi Horizonti* and *MTV* or *Muslim TV Igman.* Among these, it is likely that the newspaper *Preporod* has the most influence, as its circulation is around 23,000 copies. Meanwhile, *SAFF* – known as a more conservative and marginal paper – is quite limited in terms of circulation, with a modest 5,000 copies published biweekly. The *Muslim TV Igman* has a limited signal, mostly available in some parts of the Sarajevo suburbs and having no significant impact. See also: www.preporod.com and www.saff.ba.

circulation, the reach of television networks and overall influence on everyday social and political affairs – the secular media requires particular analytical attention.[22]

One key concept employed in the media discourse of the Bosnian Muslim religious (and political) leadership[23] is directly related to the Media Myth of Europe: the so-called 'autochthony' (or indigenousness) of Bosnian Muslims as *European* Muslims. The authenticity of their geographical existence on European soil is frequently used to confirm and support the build-up of the ethnic group as a genuinely *European* social and political identity (hence fully legitimate and politically justified in collective consciousness).[24] This modern construction process of a collective Self, in which the notion of 'Europe' is a constitutive element, induces the development of exclusive politics that reduce Bosnian Muslims' sphere of political identification to ethno-religious elements, socially constructed as essential, *territorial* and primordial. These elements are then even translated from this context to the international sphere. In other words, this is not a process confined to the country's boundaries, but extends to the international domain: a whole new vision of the European Muslim identity is being forged by the Bosnian Muslim leadership.

---

[22] The leading Bosnian daily newspaper *Dnevni Avaz*, although 'secular', is largely congruent with Muslim social and political interests, and with a circulation of up to 100,000 copies, it is more likely to have an extensive influence on Muslim consciousness than any other, specifically 'religious' paper. For example, in the period between 15 December 2006 and 10 January 2007, *Dnevni Avaz* published 183 articles directly related to religious affairs, out of which 110 referred exclusively to the Islamic Community. See the Media Plan Research on Media and Religion, 2007 (Bh. mediji i religija: prezentacija religijskih tema, crkava i vjerskih zajednica i vjerskih autoriteta').

[23] This is the case for both – the exclusively religious figures, such as the Grand Mufti and other officials of the Islamic community on the one hand, as well as for the figureheads of the leading political parties of Bosnian Muslims, such as SDA (Party for Democratic Action) and SBiH (Party for BiH) on the other.

[24] Such claims appear on a regular basis in the Muslim dominated media. See for example the transcript of the Grand Mufti's speech at the Vienna Conference on 'Islam in Europe', published in the daily newspaper *Dnevni Avaz* on 24 March 2007, p. 5.

I will try to explain this process further by referring to two significant contemporary cases that illustrate the aforementioned theoretical deliberations. The first such case is the *Declaration of European Muslims* written in 2005 by the Grand Mufti of Bosnia and Herzegovina. This document illustrates the extent to which the practice of 'European Muslim identity' described above has penetrated the Muslim community, producing indicative cultural responses to the 'Europeanisation' impulse. The second case is that of the notorious 'cartoon crisis' and its specific reception by the Muslim community of Bosnia and Herzegovina.

Case One: The 'Declaration of European Muslims'

The *Declaration of European Muslims*, published for the first time in 2005, represents the intellectual response of a Muslim cleric to the post-September 11th global political environment and the new position in which Muslims have found themselves since. The *Declaration* offers a remedy for the problems that Muslims on the borders of Europe began experiencing after the terrorist attacks in New York, Madrid and London. This remedy is presented as also extending to the future status of Muslims in Europe. It consists of a form of political 'institutionalisation' for Muslim representation in Europe, via the creation of a unified *political* subject that would represent the vast Muslim communities throughout the European Union.[25]

The *Declaration* advocates, among other things, an 'institutional [presence] of Islam in Europe; the economic development of the Muslim Community so that it may have full spiritual and cultural freedom and independence; the foundation of Islamic schools capable of educating European-born Muslims for the new challenges faced in multicultural societies; the insistence on political

---

[25] The fact that it was drafted by a Muslim cleric *outside* the EU is also analytically valuable in the given context.

freedom that will enable European Muslims to have legitimate representatives in European state parliaments; the reform of European immigration policy, which has restrictive tendencies towards Muslims; and finally, opening the way for Muslim law to be recognised in matters of personal status such as Family Law.'[26]

These principles in the Declaration deserve closer attention. First, the Declaration reveals some of the nuances in the overall Muslim response to the critical events between September 2001 in New York and July 2005 in London. Although it may seem like an attempt to open up the Muslim community towards more flexible and democratic practices, it actually promotes a sort of Muslim 'constitutional isolationism' and seeks to establish the community of Muslims in Europe as an inwardly oriented political subject. Aside from the emphasis on democracy as a universal value shared by Bosnian Muslims, the document shows signs of political and cultural contraction, associated with communitarian and culturally exclusive values. This can be inferred from the fact that the Declaration calls for the establishment of a body that will speak on behalf of all Muslims in Europe, transforming an initially *religious* identity into a *political* one that is to be carved into European political practice. In other words, it seems to call for a constitution of the European political community not as a union of *citizens,* but as a union of *believers* – categorised in accordance with their religious beliefs and sense of belonging. Thus the Declaration represents some sort of a postmodern call for the establishment of 'Westphalian public spheres', as Nancy Fraser has labelled them.[27] These

---

[26] The *Declaration of European Muslims* can be accessed at various locations online; it was first published in August 2005. The English version I use here is available at http://www.islamicpluralism.org/texts/2006t/bosnianclericsdeclaration.htm.

[27] Nancy Fraser, 'Transnationalizing the Public Sphere', in *Republicart*, multilingual web journal, http://www.republicart.net/disc/publicum/fraser01_en.htm, 2005.

consist of particularised and culturally separated public domains, with religious groups as the political foundations of society.[28]

The key characteristic that sets the Declaration within the context of the Media Myth of Europe is the fact that it tries to build its authority on the basis of the fact that it comes from Bosnian Muslims as *essentially European Muslims*. It seems to be designed to represent a true call upon Europe from Europe itself. Also, in normative terms, the Declaration uses a *minority* discourse – since the Bosnian Muslim community perceives itself as a minority in the larger European context – to establish new legitimacy for a largely *immigrant* community.[29] The Declaration advocates that the 'autochthonous' European Muslim minority should determine the rules of the game for the entire Muslim population of Europe. In a way, by implicitly claiming superior status as Muslims 'autochthonous' to (geographical) Europe, it stands on the shoulders of Orientalism and proclaims the secondary political relevance of Muslims originating from elsewhere.

Except for some rare individual cases, no substantive *critical* reception of the document has appeared in public discourse in Bosnia and Herzegovina.[30] Ample evidence of the positive and uncritical reception of the *Declaration* was the

---

[28] Paradoxically, the *Declaration* thus indirectly advocates a constitution of Europe as a dominantly Christian political community, where the rights of Muslims will be defined by their (minority) religious instead of citizenship status. In this context, the *Declaration* is a document based, in the philosophical sense, on the same social and political values exemplified in the efforts of the Vatican to incorporate exclusively Christian foundations into the Constitution of Europe.

[29] The problem is that these two – minority and immigrant – concepts of 'ethnocultural justice' very often entail different *normative* solutions. See for example Will Kymlicka, *Politics in the Vernacular: Nationalism, Multiculturalism and Citizenship* (Oxford: Oxford University Press, 2001).

[30] Although the *Declaration* was presented to the public by the Muslim weekly paper *Preporod* – followed by a series of commentaries written by different Muslim officials and thinkers – there were no substantively critical reviews of the document, nor of the suggestions and principles expressed within. This was due to the inherently subjective understanding of the *Declaration* – Mr. Aziz Kadribegović, the *Preporod* editor in chief, told me that since it was written by 'our' religious leader, no critical pieces could appear in *Preporod*; conversation with Mr. Kadribegović on 8 May 2007.

68

fact that the large majority of the leading commentators and editors in the media and members of the intellectual community – with one exception[31] – did not notice the exclusivist spirit of the Grand Mufti's *Declaration*. They did not comment on the way it had placed itself on higher ontological grounds, as an expression of self-proclaimed 'genuine European Muslims' who could speak on behalf of all European Muslims as a result of their 'European' credentials. This also applies to the discrepancy between the particularistic claims of the *Declaration* and the proclaimed universal principles of the faith as such. It seems that the ambivalent character of the document was concealed by the prevailing symbolism of 'Europe'.

Although these notions also clearly generate questions about relations between ethical universalism and its cultural-political realisation, no such analysis has appeared in the Bosnian media so far either. Instead, the media echoed the Declaration's call for political representation based on exclusively cultural characteristics, thus contributing to the reduction of faith to its political manifestation. Also, none of the media exposed the illiberal character of the *Declaration*, in its marginalisation of individuals of Muslim origin who did not want to be represented in the public space *as Muslims,* but rather as citizens of the European Union. To a large extent, the communitarian, highly exclusivist and cocooned disposition of the document was concealed behind the power of the symbolism and discourse of 'Europe'.

These uncritical interpretations of the *Declaration* reveal the media's unified attitude towards the amalgam of notions of 'Europe' and 'Islam'. It seems that even the simple positioning of such essential notions reduces the potential for critical and rational discourse and allows politics to be reduced to identity

---

[31] I refer here to the text by the Bosnian academic, Esad Duraković, published in the daily paper *Oslobođenje* on 18 March 2006, 'Krupan korak u pogrešnom pravcu' (A Giant Leap in a Wrong Direction), *Pogled*.

boundaries. The result is a form of, *cultural fundamentalism*, a practice that pushes culture into the centre of politics. In this particular case, the invocation of 'Europe' represents a cultural pattern that seeks to establish political legitimacy for those who invoke it.

Case Two: The Cartoon Controversy, Bosnian Muslims and 'Europe'

The second case considered here is the public reception of the 'cartoon crisis' and the subsequent events associated with it, which reveal further interesting details about the dominant perception of 'Europe' in Bosnia and Herzegovina. Unlike other, predominantly Muslim countries that reacted rather vehemently to the publication of cartoons by the Danish newspaper *Jyllands Posten*, Muslims in Bosnia and Herzegovina were relatively calm. A small group of believers did protest, expressing their anger in a folkloric style through the burning of European countries' flags. Apart from this, no noteworthy reaction took place. However, as anywhere else, the media reacted with stories, commentaries and reports. Analytically, two important trends emerged: firstly, most reports criticised both the publication of cartoons and the dismay violently expressed by Muslims worldwide. The decision of *Jyllands Posten* to publish the provocative cartoons was presented as an act that deepened the gap between Muslims and the West, while the violent protests were depicted as the 'wrong Muslim answer' to a provocation. Secondly, the 'cartoon case', accompanied by the repeated publication of the cartoons in other newspapers in Europe, including in neighbouring Croatia, was interpreted as a product of the modern and secular – understood as 'godless' – social environment on the one hand, and as the symbolic continuation of clashes between Islam and Christianity on the other, particularly after the Pope's notorious *Regensburg* speech.

A more sophisticated analysis shows that the general feeling, articulated more clearly by subsequently published media outlets, was not that of a Christian crusade by Europe against Muslims, but of *Europe's ignorance of its own values*.[32] This is what was deemed the cause not only of the cartoon crisis, but indirectly of the Pope's misdirected speech as well. In this view, it is not 'Europe' as an archetype of Christendom that is to be blamed for the crisis. Instead, it is *Europe's own failure to become what it is essentially supposed to be* – the unquestionable good that transcends historical experience.[33] This collective, some might say Platonian, feeling thus generated a certain disappointment in 'Europe' among Bosnian Muslims, also driven by the sense of betrayal at Europe's failure to prevent the genocide in Srebrenica. However, that was soon to be changed by the prevailing symbolic power of its meaning – this time with Islam as a means of 'Europe's great return to itself'. This was expressed through various appearances and comments by clerics in the media. One of them, made again by the Grand Mufti, is interesting:

> [a]wakened, Islam began to remind Europe and Christianity of their common spiritual values of the Abrahamic tradition. Muslims in

---

[32] This was expressed, for example, in an interview the Grand Mufti gave to the Croatian *Jutarnji list*, which was later re-published by the Bosnian Muslim News Agency (MINA) on 23 September 2006.

It can be found at: http://www.preporod.com/index.php?option=com_content&task=view&id=124&Itemid=100. See also the article published in *BH Dani* Magazine, entitled 'The Clash of Civilizations?', 10 February 2006. I must emphasise that this phenomenon is not limited to the Balkan Muslim community: similar understandings are prevalent in other monotheistic communities as well. An interesting example is the following statement, made by a Serbian Orthodox Provincial, Amfilohije Radović: 'Europe is not against us because we do not want to be Europe … but because we are, not by our merit, but by the gift of God, the keepers of a genuine Jerusalemic-Mediterranean Europeanness, that doesn't accept the loss of the balance between human existence at the crossroads on one side, and the horizontality and verticality of the Honourable Cross on the other. The West is too focused on the material world; it deifies its own acts through expansion and totalitarianism of the worst kind. Greed and the profane mind are its religion.' Ivan Čolović, *Politika simbola: ogledi o političkoj antropologiji*, [*The Politics of Symbols: Essays on Political Anthropology*] XX Vek: Beograd, 2003, p. 53.

[33] Similar views were expressed by the Sarajevo *alim* Mustafa Spahić, when he said: 'I see the cartoons that appeared in that Danish newspaper as a betrayal of the European tradition, a blasphemy shaped as freedom'. See *BH Dani* Magazine, 10 February 2006, p. 36.

Europe require more places for worship now, so seeing them praying on the streets and in the parks of London and Paris is not a rare case at all, while the churches stay empty. It seems that the European Christians got used to a life without God and without the Church. So Islam has 'shaken' Europe, not in the sense of a clash between Christianity and Islam, but in the sense of reminding them of faith as a value forgotten by most Europeans. I think Pope Benedict's speech in Regensburg was more of a protest against 'godless' Europe than against 'evil and inhumane' Islam, but, being more aware than others, Muslims have reacted in a way that had veiled the core of the Pope's message – which says that the times of European atheism have passed, and it is time for Europeans to return to God.[34]

Having discussed the cartoon crisis, we have seen that the reaction among many Muslims worldwide added or reinforced an anti-Islamic stigma to the very meaning of 'Europe'. Meanwhile, the media discourse put forward by Bosnian Muslim leaders and journalists understood 'Europe' as flawed only from the current, historically relative perspective. Its ontological values remained intact. According to this kind of interpretation, the mission of Islam is to awaken 'Europe' and help it return to its forgotten, better Self.

Conclusion

In summarising, we can distinguish between the *causes* and *consequences* of the Media Myth of 'Europe' in Bosnia's Muslim community. *The causes*, to some extent, reflect the specific position of Bosnia and Herzegovina and its Muslims towards Europe. A former colonial power has turned into a founding pillar of

---

[34]   *Preporod*, 31 October 2006.

72

the country's modern existence. Instead of the clash between 'Christian' Europe and 'Muslim' Bosnia that had characterised these relations at the end of the nineteenth century, a new relationship has been established. This relationship serves the needs of both: the Bosnian Muslim community seeks to position itself as a distinct ethnic nation in the European context and ensure stability linking the country to the EU as a geopolitical power. Meanwhile, the European Union aims to stabilise the fragile Balkan region and incorporate a largely 'westernised' community of Muslims into its alliance. The dichotomy of 'tradition' vs. 'modernity' in which the relations of Bosnian Muslims and Europe were originally created has diminished over the course of history, peaking with the coming of globalisation and the opening up of the Balkans to western cultural, social and political influence. Thus the new geopolitical setting has induced a shift in the perception of 'Europe', from a colonial threat to a foundation of Bosnian Muslim identity's international legitimacy.

The causes of the production of the Media Myth of Europe are also to be found within the modern ideology of nation building, which has introduced essentialist categories into the social construction of identity.[35] The Bosnian Muslim community – discovering its own ethnicity – has followed this trajectory of essentialist identity construction. Paradoxically, it was the modernity of nation building which first brought primordial arguments into the arena of politics, including the construction of 'Europe' as a key identification point of the ethnic nation in the making. Media discourse, throughout different political persuasions, has been positive and uncritical towards this symbolism of 'Europe'. It has thereby carried such essentialist concepts into the core of public communication, and merged the desired and programmatic values into a

---

[35] Benedict Anderson, *Imagined Communities: Reflection of the Origin and Spread of Nationalism* (London: Verso, 1991); Eric Hobsbawm, *Nations and Nationalism since 1780: Programme, Myth, Reality* (Cambridge: Cambridge University Press, 1990); Anthony Smith, *Nationalism and Modernism* (New York: Routledge, 1998).

single ideological narrative of Europe and Bosnian as essentially *European Muslims*.

A political myth, as Girardet has shown, aims to create new patterns of social organisation.[36] It is never haphazard or born out of nothing. It always seeks to (re)establish or (re)constitute particular relations of social and political power or to (re)craft an identity. Given this, *the consequences* of the Myth of Europe can be said to have contributed to the creation of the Bosnian Muslim community as an ethnic nation (Bosniaks) on the bases of essentialist categories of cultural belonging. These categories were imported from the West, especially after the 'cultural turn' in the second half of the twentieth century that introduced a shift of emphasis towards *meaning* and matters of culture, and away from those of politics or economy. This shift contributed to the building of an identity narrative on claims of indigenousness ('autochthony') and territoriality, initiating the usage of the symbolism of 'Europe' to establish the identity's legitimacy in the wider political context. In order to best harness it as a symbolic resource in the construction of Bosnian Muslim identity, 'Europe' has been turned into an essentialist category, bringing about a specific transposition of 'Europe' and 'Islam' in Bosnia and Herzegovina. For Bosnian Muslims, 'Europe' now represents an integral part of their identity, and a form of unquestionable, sacred and essentially anti-secular symbolic practice. Thus both 'Islam' and 'Europe' have been transformed in this process: 'Islam' as a religion has been *secularised* and reduced to a dimension of political identity, while 'Europe' has been *sacralised* and almost elevated from political concept to a form of religion.

This basically means that in contemporary Bosnia and Herzegovina, both 'Europe' and 'Islam' are to a significant extent media constructs. In the

---

[36] Girardet, *Mythes*, p. 213.

74

country's transitional context in which notions of identity prevail over other social issues, media features are abundant with symbolism of 'Europe' and 'Islam', both serving communitarian needs to differentiate, identify and categorise. The way 'Europe' and 'Islam' are being represented in the media determines the public patterns of understanding of these concepts. Their meaning is thus dependent on the context in which the media act as one of the principal subjects of identity production, aiding the political efforts to create, legitimise and promote particular identities in the public sphere. Thus it can be inferred that the notions of 'Europe' and 'Islam' in contemporary Bosnia and Herzegovina are no more than symbolic elements of (mainly) ethnic boundaries, asserted by both political and religious leaders.

The key political and philosophical problem with this matrix of media representation of 'Europe' and 'Islam' in Bosnia and Herzegovina is that it *reduces the polity to community,* and sidelines the importance of people as *individuals.* This matrix contributes further to the perpetuation of a social system in which collective representations, created to differentiate identities and ensure ethno-religious legitimacy in political contexts, dominate over a reflexive and dialogical understanding of contemporary social and political complexities. Instead 'Europe' and 'Islam' being understood as contingencies prone to contextual transformation, they are being perceived exclusively as categories of rootedness and belonging. The tension between community and individuality remains unresolved, with the former dominating the latter.

Aside from the theoretical claim about the prevalence of communitarian understandings of 'Europe' and 'Islam', the examples above point to other facts worth highlighting. First, they illustrate the different responses of the Muslim community to contemporary challenges pertaining to relations between Muslims and Europe. Bosnian Muslims have a distinct and complex understanding of 'Europe', mainly due to specific historical experiences in which European powers played the roles of imperial colonisers as well as modernisers of the once underdeveloped, rural and feudal country. The original dichotomy of tradition vs. modernity – in which Europe stood as a modern force aiming to supplant traditional (Muslim) sources of identification with its own system of (Christian) values –diminished over the course of history, in favour of the modernity to which Bosnian Muslims tie their social and political visions. Instead of the identity's adversary, 'Europe' was transformed into one the key foundations of the Bosnian Muslims' *ethnicity* and elevated as a supreme metaphor for social and political good. It is this setting that prevented the creation of the deep ruptures between Muslims and Europe that were visible in other Muslim-populated countries in cases of events such as the cartoon controversy or the Pope's *Regensburg* speech. It also neutralised the possible 'clash of civilisations' rhetoric that could have risen among radical activists.

Secondly, the case shows how much this relationship is dependent upon the dominant media discourse and the ways in which symbols of 'Europe' and 'Islam' are wielded for political purposes. Obviously, the media power can have a decisive influence on identity creation.[37] If the context allows such loops, foes can easily be transformed into friends, and adversaries into allies. The Bosnian Muslim appropriation of 'Europe' is an example of such a transposition, in which group identity interests determine the character of symbols employed in the public sphere. Once 'Europe' had turned into a useful tool for drawing new identity boundaries, it ceased to be a symbol of the distant adversary which one opposes.

Finally, and most importantly, the case of Bosnian Muslims shows to what extent the relationship between Muslims and Europe is *historically contingent*.

---

[37] Benedict Anderson was among the first ones to show this. See Anderson, *Imagined Communities*, 1990.

Once an enemy that had wanted to assimilate Bosnian Muslims into European Christendom, 'Europe' has been transformed into a symbol of the Bosnian Muslims' authenticity. The case of Bosnia and Herzegovina thus offers a clear example of an anti-essentialist reading of the 'nature' of the European-Muslim relationship. It shows that 'Muslims' and 'Europe' are not ontological adversaries, but contingent collective *representations* intertwined in a common historical context.

These conclusions make Bosnia and Herzegovina not only an interesting example but also a certain 'laboratory' for future explorations of identity layers and relationships in which even notorious adversaries, such as 'Islam' and 'Europe', can be seen in a totally different perspective.

Chapter Four

Beyond Government Control: Divergent Views on Europe in the Egyptian Media

Hanaa Ebeid

It is widely held that media outlets in the Arab world are all under government control, and that freedom of expression is very limited or non-existent. A corollary of this view is that media representations of different international actors and issues stem necessarily from official state positions. Exaggeration or silence in coverage would therefore shape the public opinion in line with official positions especially in matters of foreign affairs. The reality, however, appears to be much more nuanced. Naomi Sakr, editor of *Arab Media and Political Renewal: Community, Legitimacy and Public Life*, rightly argues that the notion that opinion can be shaped according to media coverage downplays the experience of individuals and communities, and their role in shaping public opinion. She explains further that the more choice readers and viewers have, the more the media have to cater to public opinion.[1]

More importantly, there is considerable diversity among Arab countries in terms of media freedom. In his study of mass media in 18 Arab countries, William Rugh classifies Arab media into four categories – mobilisation media, loyalist media, diverse media and transition media. Egypt lies in the last of the four.

Mellor goes even further, suggesting a more open relationship between the Arab media and public opinion, whereby the media plays an important role in setting the public agenda and framing news. This is specifically evident in Arab

---

[1]   Naomi Sakr, ed., *Arab Media and Political Renewal: Community, Legitimacy and Public Life* (London: I.B. Tauris, 2007), pp. 1-5.

countries enjoying a deep rooted professional tradition. Particular examples are the Lebanese and Egyptian press, which date back to the second half of the nineteenth century.[2]

Hence, despite significant governmental influence over the media, there is more diversity in the Arab media than the stereotype suggests. In general, the Arab media have come to reflect the diversity of actors and wide range of opinions within the Arab world itself. Even state-controlled media cannot be detached from public opinion, and they often reflect a relatively independent line. The advent of privately owned media channels, most notably satellite television, and privately owned newspapers in the 1990s has led to a considerable liberalisation of the media throughout the region. However, an assessment of the impact of new and independent media and an analysis of their trends in representation is premature. Most often, it can only be based on observation and not empirical studies, due to the short time that has elapsed since the introduction of these new media outlets to the public sphere.[3]

A second corollary of the conventional wisdom about Arab media which needs to be reconsidered is the idea that media liberalisation automatically leads to more favourable representations of the West. The main hypothesis here is that political regimes manipulate the media to channel public sentiment against foreign actors, especially at times of crisis. However, the case of the Egyptian media demonstrates that more liberalisation does not necessarily lead to better representations of the West as a general rule. Representation, in this regard, is contingent upon many factors: when cultural matters are at stake,

---

[2]   Noha Mellor, *The Making of Arab News*, (Lanham MD: Rowman and Littlefield, 2005) cited in Adel Iskandar, 'Lines in the Sand: Problematizing Arab Media in the Post Taxonomic Era,' *Arab Media and Society*, http://www.arabmediasociety.com/topics/index. php?t_article=145&p=1

[3]   For a review of different trends in assessing the impact of new media, see Jacob Skovgaard-Petersen, 'Democratization and the New Media,' in Dietrich Jung ed., *Democratization and Development. New Political Strategies for the New Middle East*, (New York: Palgrave Macmillan, 2006), pp. 87-88.

private media channels respond mainly to an alienated or angry public, and reflect negative perceptions of Europe and/or the West, as compared to state-controlled or state-affiliated media. This does not necessarily reflect an official position or preference, but could be the result of the predominantly secular nature of the state-affiliated print media, and the individual or collective ideological beliefs of these media professionals.

Thus the dynamics of the Egyptian media are far more complex than the conventional wisdom would suggest. This is partly the result of the origins and historical evolution of print press in Egypt, whereby the press has been closely related to the national movement, and often voiced the political and intellectual elites' quest for modernity and national liberation. The role of the media in this sense probes the question of whether it acts as a Habermasian public sphere.

Media messages are determined by a subtle arrangement, in which media outlets and media professionals interact with public opinion within a particular political context – these factors together affect the overall outlook on concepts of Self and Other. The interplay of several factors affect media coverage, including the nature, ownership and evolution of the media outlet, public opinion and the political context. As regards Europe's representation in Egyptian media, one of the main influential factors which is generally downplayed concerns the particularities of Egyptian-European relations, and the outlook of the Egyptian elite towards Europe. The latter tends to produce a positive representation of Europe – if a vulnerable one. There are several factors at work here.

Firstly, Egypt is a country which does not aspire to membership of the European Union (EU), but which is at the same time one of the largest beneficiaries of EU funds. Consequently, Europe is mainly perceived as a benevolent global power and as an ally, commensurate with Egyptian stature.

Partnership with the European Union is mainly envisioned as a zone for mutual prosperity.

Cultural ties with Europe assume a lower profile in media representations of Europe. There is not a straightforwardly positive representation of mutual affinity, nor a polarised one of Europe as cultural 'Other'. However, this state of affairs has recently been changing, giving way to a more negative representation of Europe in the aftermath of the Danish 'cartoon crisis'. It remains to be seen whether these changes will prove to be enduring.

Finally, the 'American factor' is an intervening variable which complicates Europe's image among Arab audiences. For public opinion in Egypt, evidence of Euro-American congruence in policy positions, especially after the war on Iraq, have impacted upon Europe's image negatively.

As a rule then, defining 'Europe' in terms of political alliance and economic utility underlies a positive representation of Europe in general. However, this positive image of Europe's global role is subject to cyclical fluctuations in response to regional developments and cultural sensitivities.

The Media as an Agent of Representation

The media plays a highly influential role in the Egyptian public domain. Media outlets are far from neutral agents; rather, the profile and ideological preferences of media professionals significantly shape the representations they produce. In light of this, the prominent role played by the media in Egypt can be explained by examining the media's deep rooted traditions and the role it played historically in the national movement.

Egypt was among the first countries in the Middle East to host a print press. The first papers in Egypt were published in the late eighteenth century, at the time of the French invasion. The first example of genuinely Egyptian print media emerged in the second quarter of the nineteenth century: this was an official paper published by Mohamed Ali. It was followed by another official paper, *Al-Waqa'i Al-Masreya* ('Egyptian Events'), which started in 1828 and exists to this day. In the late nineteenth and early twentieth century, private press flourished in Egypt. It was closely linked to the national liberation movement, especially during the 'liberal era', before the July Revolution of 1952.[4]

After the 1952 revolution, political parties and thus the opposition press were banned. The revolutionary regime also used censorship to monitor and control the media. It issued new papers and resumed publishing others. With the reintroduction of political parties in the mid-seventies, opposition party papers reappeared. The overall scope of freedom of expression expanded in an incremental, non-linear fashion. Meanwhile, television was introduced in Egypt during the Nasserite era in July 1960. Broadcasting and television were owned and run by a public association.

New media began to spread in Egypt in the late 1990s. These comprised privately owned newspapers and satellite channels, which enjoyed higher levels of freedom compared to national print press and television. The first satellite channels were state-owned: the Egyptian Satellite Channel was launched in 1990, and was followed by twenty channels, all owned and run by the National Union of Television and Broadcasting. Starting in 2001, nine satellite channels were launched which were jointly owned by public and private entities, but run entirely by the latter. The scope of freedom enjoyed by these channels is higher compared with national television, but they are

---

[4] Ahmed Abdel Hafeeth, 'The Legal Framework of the Egyptian Press,' in Ahmed Menessy ed., *The Media and Political Reform in Egypt*, (Cairo: Al-Ahram Centre for Political and Strategic Studies, 2007), pp. 41–44.

subject to legal and other, more subtle constraints, such as licensing procedures and the 'charter of honour', or the media code of ethics.[5]

Private print media emerged a few years earlier, with *Al-Midan* in 1995, the first private newspaper to be licensed by the Higher Council for the Press. According to the last statement of the council, there were eighteen private papers in Egypt in 2005, established and owned by shared asset companies. They were all subject to similar sets of regulations as the private satellite channels, but to a harsher penal code, which stipulates imprisonment for 'print crimes'.[6]

Very few empirical studies have directly analysed the inclinations of Egyptian media professionals towards Europe. Among these is an opinion poll conducted by the Al-Ahram Centre for Political and Strategic Studies in 2000,[7] which reflected a generally positive media outlook towards Europe, especially in economic terms. According to the poll, media professionals emerged as the group most cautious and pessimistic regarding economic liberalisation and Egypt's membership of the World Trade Organisation. However, media professionals seemed more receptive of regional integration initiatives, especially the Euro-Mediterranean Partnership (EMP).[8] In this respect, the EMP emerged as the second most preferred alternative among media circles for regional integration, following Arab integration. The EMP's credibility as a

---

[5] Essam Eldin Mohamed Hassan, 'The State of Audio and Visual Media in Egypt,' in Essam Eldin Mohamed ed., *Media in the Arab World; Between Liberalisation and Reproducing Hegemony*, (Cairo: Cairo Institute for Human Rights Studies, 2007), pp. 120-124.

[6] Mohamed Shouman, 'Independent Press and the Issue of Democracy,' in Menessy, *Media and Political Reform*, p. 17.

[7] Gamal Soltan et al, 'The Arab Polls: Egyptian Public Opinion towards Economic Conditions and Regional Integration,' *Al-Ahram*, 18 June 2001. The poll did not include questions on non-economic aspects of the EMP and was conducted before the introduction of most independent and privately owned media outlets. However the analysis remains valid in principal since the new media draws mainly from the same pool of professionals, although with better representation of younger professionals.

[8] The Euro-Mediterranean Partnership (or Barcelona Process) started in 1995 with the Barcelona Euro-Mediterranean Conference. It was organised by the European Union to strengthen its relations with the countries in the Mashriq and Maghreb regions.

viable alternative, however, exceeded that of Arab regionalism, which was ideologically and emotionally favoured.

Europe in the Media: General Trends

The following analysis focuses on print media, with special emphasis on the *Al-Ahram* daily, and some opposition party papers. The emphasis on *Al-Ahram* is attributed to a number of factors: first *Al-Ahram* is the largest daily distributed in Egypt, and its readership is estimated at half a million copies, almost three times that of the next most widely read independent daily[9]. Second, *Al-Ahram* provides the most extensive coverage of foreign affairs, while most other print media, especially private and independent papers and opposition papers, focus mainly on domestic issues. Hence *Al-Ahram* offers the most extensive coverage of Europe in its news and editorial sections, allowing for a credible analysis in this chapter, whereas media coverage of Europe in most other media outlets is limited.

Although it is problematic to draw a line between the influence of the ownership and the editorial policy or professional tradition in state-owned media including *Al-Ahram*, the diversity and trends of coverage of foreign affairs generally deflect the notion of complete correlation with state views. Moreover, the long history of *Al-Ahram*, which was established in 1875, exemplifies Mellor's argument about deep-rooted professional traditions in the Egyptian and Lebanese press.[10] *Al-Ahram* has long maintained increased attention to foreign affairs: its editorial policy has been documented as favouring France during the decades of British colonisation for example.[11] Attention to foreign affairs –especially compared to other media outlets, print

---

[9]   Precise distribution figures are not available.
[10] Noha Mellor, *Making of Arab News*, 2005.
[11] Soheir Iskandar, *The Egyptian Press and National Issues 1946-1954*, (Cairo: The Egyptian National Book Association, 1992), pp. 71-77.

and non-print – has persisted to date, as well-resourced foreign bureaus have allowed *Al-Ahram* a noticeable edge. The time frame of this analysis focuses on the aftermath of the Bush Administration with special emphasis on the onset of the war in Iraq, where Europe's media representation was defined in contrast with the US.

However, allusions will be made to the 'new media' – the privately owned satellite channels and newspapers, especially the *Al-Masry Al-Youm* paper – when they offer a distinct pattern of representation, for the sake of comparison. As regards the private print media, attention will be drawn to Europe's representation as a pro-reform power, in light of the natural interest of new media in domestic issues and particularly political reform. Meanwhile, the analysis of private satellite channels will focus on the Danish cartoons episode, due to the role played by some talk shows in mobilising the public for economic boycott. It should be noted that the references to independent and private media are not tackled in a strictly comparative sense because of their different time frames, as some of the issues covered date before the establishment of private media in Egypt.

This analysis will not include online publications or blogs. However, it is noteworthy that among the 100 'most visited' websites in Egypt are the electronic versions of the dailies included in the analysis, the foremost among which is *Al-Ahram*, in 25th place, followed by the independent *Al-Masry Al-Youm*, ranking 30th. The analysis also excludes the Muslim Brotherhood, since their media representation of Europe is mostly undifferentiated from what depictions of 'the west' as cultural 'other'.

As a point of departure, it is important to emphasise the fact that the Egyptian media coverage of Europe is overall limited. This is acknowledged by Lucarelli and Fioramonti's survey of the EU's external image.[12] Apart from the national dailies, and particularly *Al-Ahram*, media attention is scant when it comes to Europe, and representations are sparse, eclectic and often inconsistent. State-affiliated media give much more coverage to foreign affairs compared to opposition and private media. The fact that new and independent media pay little attention to foreign affairs and actors has been highlighted by a number of scholars.[13]

Nevertheless, several trends in representations of Europe can still be traced, particularly in the print media. Firstly, the level of attention paid to Europe – gauged in terms of the volume of coverage – comes second after that paid to the United States (US), which is regarded as the leading international actor among other great powers. The media's tone on Europe and the European Union is more positive across different media outlets than their tone on the US.

Secondly, representations of Europe focus on the European Union's internal developments, as well as political and economic relations with the Middle East and Egypt. The visits and statements of European Union officials are highlighted extensively through front page coverage in national dailies, especially when official opinions held in common with Egypt are expressed. Interest in European internal developments, especially towards integration, are tackled almost in a celebratory manner, suggesting that the positive outlook towards Europe goes beyond the echoing of official positions.

Thirdly, the coverage of Europe consists mostly of political news, official statements, and economic analyses. Opinion articles and editorials are

---

[12]   Florenzo Fioramonti and Sonia Lucarelli, 'The EU Viewed by the Others; Drawing Some Conclusions', in *The External Image of the European Union,* Forum on the Problems of Peace and War, Garnet, at
http://www.garnet-eu.org/fileadmin/documents/working_papers/1707/15%20Conclusions.pdf
[13]   See for example, Kenneth Cooper, 'Politics and Priorities: Inside the Egyptian Press,' *Arab Media and Society,* at http://www.arabmediasociety.com/?article=689

triggered by occasional upsurges in interest in response to internal developments in Europe, or bilateral and regional relations, generally attributable to the political role of Europe in the Middle East.

Fourthly, terms of reference vary according to the topic of representation: where economic relations are considered, the Euro-Mediterranean Partnership is the main term of reference, thus equating Europe with the EU, whereas political representations of Europe pay little if any homage to the partnership.

Beyond national dailies, concern with Europe in general and the EMP in particular is much less pronounced, but the overall outlook remains similar. For instance, the editorial policy towards Europe of *Al-Wafd* daily – mouthpiece of the liberal *Al-Wafd* opposition party – is similar to that of *Al-Ahram*, despite less coverage and opinion articles. Surprisingly enough, in response to Europe's political reform agenda or condemnations of Egypt's human rights record, private and opposition media representations of Europe are no less critical than the national or state-owned media.

Unbundling the Image[14]

Within these general trends in the media representation of Europe, there is considerable variation, due to important changes over the past years. These are now considered individually.

Europe as political ally or colonial power?

There is a considerable consensus in print and especially state-affiliated media representations of Europe on its status as a political ally and an even broker in the Arab-Israeli conflict. In this respect, European foreign policy representatives to the Middle East, and particularly High Representative for the Common Foreign and Security Policy Javier Solana, are in general

---

[14] Compare also 'The Partnership in Southern Eyes: Reflections on the Discourse in the Egyptian Media', *EuroMeSCo papers*, No. 27, October 2004.

appreciated. Often the mere presence of a European representative is considered positive. The activities and visits of European officials are given intensive coverage, especially when congruence of opinion is voiced. This trend has particularly prevailed since the beginning of the Bush administration's term in office, and more specifically in the aftermath of September 11th, with the rise of discontent with US policies in the region. Europe has been increasingly represented as the moral power, or the international actor that respects multilateralism and international legitimacy.

Indeed, the general trend in the political representation of Europe has seen increased importance attached to areas of political congruence, which are generally highlighted and sometimes exaggerated, while policy differences are tolerated less, and trigger sharp media criticism.

In this regard, European condemnations of Israeli policies are extensively covered. For example, when the October 2003 Flash Eurobarometer survey, carried out for the European Commission in the fifteen member states of the EU, found that nearly 60 percent of European citizens believe Israel poses the greatest threat to world peace, this was highlighted and welcomed.[15] Identifying with Europe in the context of the Arab-Israeli conflict can involve going as far as considering Israel the main obstacle to European global power status.[16]

This positive representation of Europe has surged during periods in which the peace process was ongoing or in response to windows of hope of reinvigorating the peace process. However, the eventual halt of the peace process has led to

---

[15]   Salama Ahmed Salama, 'Israel in European Eyes,' Al-Ahram, 5 November 2003; Hani Assal, 'The European Union and the Poll Paradox,' Al-Ahram, 7 November 2003; 'Europe Defies the Holocaust Guilt,' Al-Ahram, 22 November 2003; Salama, 'Anti Semitism,' Al-Ahram, 23 November 2003.

[16]   Emad Gad, 'Anti Semitism: European Attempts to Counter Blackmail,' Al-Ahram, 18 June 2002; Abdel A'ati Mohamed, 'For Europe to Confront Israel,' Al-Ahram, 25 February 2003; Mohamed El Samak, 'Israel Between the US and Europe,' Al-Ahram, 19 February 2003.

what might be termed a 'collective disappointment' in the Arab world.[17] This has had a negative impact on the political representation of Europe which resounds in the Arab media.

Whenever there have been increased expectations of Europe becoming 'the power for world justice', followed by disappointment, these have usually been led to more intense disillusionment. On these occasions, negative representations of Europe resonate in opinion editorials, with titles such as 'Europe's impotence',[18] 'Europe does not have the courage',[19] 'Where is the European Role?',[20] and 'The myth of the European Role.'[21] Such articles lament Europe's inability to deliver its perceived role in the region 'in a moment of American hegemony'.[22]

Cases of incongruence in European positions or policies on the one hand, and what are perceived to be Arab rights or positions on the other, are less readily tolerated in the media. The European Union's list of terrorist organisations, which was first welcomed for 'ameliorating the American list' for instance,[23] was harshly criticised when the Palestinian group HAMAS was later included. There was an outburst of anger at this 'unexpected' move on Europe's part, followed by a plethora of opinion editorials condemning it as a compromise of Palestinian rights. The authors saw Europe as bowing to American pressures,[24] and even as supporting Israeli state terrorism by confiscating the Palestinian right of self-defence.[25]

---

[17] Mohamed Sabrin, 'Not a Myth: The future of EU Role and the Peace Settlement: Interview with Miguel Moratinos', Al-Ahram, 31 July 2001.
[18] Salama, 'Europe's Impotence,' Al-Ahram, 9 April 2002.
[19] Ibid., 'Europe Does not have the Courage,' Al-Ahram, 19 June 2001.
[20] Ibid., 'Where is the European Role?,' Al-Ahram, 1 May 2001.
[21] Mohamed Sabrin, 'Not a Myth: The Role of the EU, interview', Al-Ahram, 31 July 2001.
[22] Nabil Fahmy, 'The Moment of Truth,' Al-Ahram, 18 February 2003.
[23] Necola Nasif, Al-Nahar, quoted in Al-Ahram, 4 January 2004.
[24] Ahmed El Berri, 'Uprising Intifada or Terrorism,' Al-Ahram, 13 December 2001.
[25] Amr El Shobaky, 'European Support for Israeli Terrorism,' Al-Ahram, 16 September 2003.

Such instances usually strengthen the anti-western stream in the media, which lumps Europe and the US together in one hostile camp. This trend, though less widely articulated, views the European role in the region with scepticism, and identifies it with the colonial experience. It represents Europe as 'unwilling to take clear stances against Israel, and making do with verbal condemnations.'[26]

The 'American factor' has been significant in shaping Egyptian media representations of Europe. Differences across the Atlantic over policies in the Middle East have been a characteristic determinant of Europe's image in Egyptian media. The Euro-American 'rift' has been taken to include policy issues as varied as the Kyoto Protocol, the Arab-Israeli conflict, the war on Iraq, and even economic policy differences, as seen in the debate on genetically modified food. The image in the media has indeed been one of an Atlantic relationship in crisis, and of Europe as the fairer power.

Even some traditional Eurosceptics in the media highlighted the differences in positions between the United States and Europe, and praised the latter, especially before the war on Iraq.[27] European criticism of President Bush's first declaration of the notion of the 'axis of evil' was underscored, through extensive coverage of statements by European leaders, as well as opinion articles and political analyses.[28] In this regard, the overwhelming representation of Europe was that of an important political, if not a military power.[29]

Just prior to the war on Iraq, Egyptian media phrased Euro-American differences in terms of a deep, structural EU-US rift, and opinion polls in

---

[26] Salama, 'Illusionary Alternatives,' *Al-Ahram*, 13 January 2002; 'The Myth of European Impotence', *Al-Ahram*, 19 April 2002.

[27] Salama, 'America is Lonely,' *Al-Ahram*, 21 February 2002.

[28] Gad, 'The European Vision of the Axis of Evil Notion,' *Al-Ahram*, 23 February 2002; Taha El Magdoub, 'Europe and American Unilateralism,' *Al-Ahram*, 5 June 2002; 'America and Europe, Allies or Aliens,' 3 June 2002.

[29] Abdel Azim Hamad,' America Does Not Need Europe Militarily, but Cannot Go It Alone Politically,' *Al-Ahram*, 16 March 2002.

European countries opposing American foreign policy were the focus of both news briefs and opinion articles.[30] Once the war on Iraq began, despite the active involvement of Britain and other European countries, the representation of Europe remained focused on French and German opposition to it. A less prevalent trend characteristic of a few opposition paper opinion articles – liberal and leftist alike – cited neo colonialism and the concept of new crusades.[31]

Meanwhile, the French and German anti-war positions led some of the Eurosceptics to welcome Europe's position on the war on Iraq,[32] and its role in opposing US military intervention schemes and 'imperial aspirations'.[33] The image of Europe was thus credited as mindful of Arab rights and positions on the one hand, and of international legitimacy and respect for the United Nations on the other. This came at a time when American respect for both had hit its lowest point.[34]

In this context, advances in European defence policy and common foreign and security policies were generally welcomed as a counterbalance to that of NATO, which was open to manipulation by unilateral American interests. Developments towards establishing a European force independent from NATO were depicted as representing a rift in trans-Atlantic relations. [35]

As far as the war on Iraq's impact was concerned, then, the pre-war phase helped consolidate a positive representation of Europe. Media coverage focused on the congruence in Arab-European stances, and on consolidating

---

[30]   Hazem Abdel Rahman, 'Europe Opposes Bush,' *Al-Ahram*, 22 August 2001; 'Germany and France Against America,' *Al-Ahram*, 19 February 2003.
[31]   Abbas El Tarabili, 'Homoum Masreya,' *Al-Wafd*, 19 March 2004.
[32]   Salama, 'Europe Says No,' *Al-Ahram*, 19 January 2003.
[33]   Salwa Habib, 'The Axis of Nuisance,' *Al-Ahram*, 2 February 2003; El Sayed Yassin, 'The Global Defiance to Empire,' *Al-Ahram*, 20 February 2003.
[34]   Mohi Eddin El Ashmawy, 'The Positions of France, Germany, Russia and China in the Iraqi Crisis support International Law and the UN Charter,' *Al-Ahram*, 19 March 2003.
[35]   Said El Lawendi, 'The Cross-Atlantic Rift Escalates,' *Al-Ahram*, 11 May 2003.

trust in the European role in the region, synonymous in most media channels with the Franco-German stance. Aside from mainstream applause for the European position on the Iraq war, there were other, less pertinent trends in the media, and particularly that of the opposition. These media perceived the war as an act of neocolonialism, and brought to the debate historical references to European colonialism, the establishment of the state of Israel and the Sykes-Picot agreements which drew up the states of Syria, Jordan, Lebanon, and Palestine, and paved the way for the British mandate over Palestine.[36] When Europe failed to stop the war on Iraq, the tone was predictably negative, blaming Europe for its 'lame role', and for disappointing Arab expectations of Europe being a reliable great power, 'free' of American hegemony.[37]

Hence, as viewed in the media, the war on Iraq was mainly perceived as a litmus test for Europe's 'ability' to escape American hegemony,[38] and to reverse America's declared intentions of war.[39] It was followed by disappointment when the European role failed to meet Arab expectations regarding stopping the war.

The evolution in media political representations of Europe has been influenced most by the international and regional context, and the American factor has been the most visible in shaping representations of Europe since September 11th and the war on Iraq. Against this troubled backdrop, Europe's image has swung between two extremes; the natural political ally and benevolent power on the one hand, and the ex-colonial power on the other. Whether either position took precedence was contingent on the political context. Hence the positive political representation of Europe is subject to reversals following

---

[36] 'The English-American Coordination: Old Balfour-New Balfour', *Al-Wafd*, 22 April 2004; Essam Kamel, 'The Very Big Middle East,' *Al-Wafd*, 24 February 2004.
[37] Salama, 'Can Europe Be Free?' *Al-Ahram*, 6 May 2003.
[38] El Lawendi, *Al-Ahram*, 11 February 2003.
[39] Mohamed El Sayed Said, 'The Remaining Hope to Save Iraq,' *Al-Ahram*, 24 February 2003.

what could be called an expectation/disappointment pattern. Whenever Europe fails the expectations of the 'ideal' power, the positive image is reversed into one of a 'lame' power. There is also a problem of favourability or rating, whereby Europe ranks second, in emotional terms, compared with natural affinities to the Arab world, and according to some 'utilitarian' accounts, particularly limited liberal voices which represent the US as the more 'capable' power.

Europe as economic partner or Leviathan?

The mainstream media representation of Europe in economic matters is also positive, and more consistently so than its political representation. In this regard, Europe is generally represented as a facilitator of Egyptian modernisation and development. In national media, this is closely related to the positive official discourse that has been extended to the Euro-Mediterranean Partnership. However, it is also attributable to media professionals' deep confidence in Europe as a zone of prosperity. There is a measure of criticism from sceptics of economic liberalisation, as well as from stakeholders of industries and economic sectors expected to suffer in case of fully liberalised trade with Europe. Nevertheless, the general discussion focuses on promises and opportunities. This incentivist discourse represents Europe as a benefactor to, and source of leverage for the development of the Egyptian economy. This was especially true at the early stages of the Barcelona process, when the hopes for a resolution to the Palestinian conflict resulted in a generally hopeful mood.

Europe's media representation in economic matters revolves around two main images: Europe as a model for economic integration and as a zone of co-prosperity. With regards to the Barcelona process, for instance, national media channels strongly echoed the official discourse envisioning the partnership with Europe as a 'necessary' phase in the overall process of 'modernising

Egypt'.[40]   In this respect, Europe has been represented as a source of investments, as well as a vast potential market.[41]

Beyond strict economic utility, an emotional value is attributed to Europe in mainstream media representations of economic matters. In this context, the EU is perceived as a model for would-be Arab regional integration. Extensive coverage of EU internal developments – such as negotiations seeking a common European Union, the establishment of a unified currency, negotiation of the Unified Constitution and most recently the Lisbon Agreement – take on an implicitly celebratory tone. Europe's growing power is at once represented as counter-balancing United States hegemony, and as a model in action for successful regional integration in a region long plagued by war.

The contrast between successful European integration and Arab disintegration resonates in most analyses on Europe. This is quite noticeable when there are internal developments in the EU towards more integration politically or economically, which are usually phrased in terms of 'lessons' for Arab integration.[42] Thus the declaration of the unified European currency was welcomed in the media, while the lost Arab 'dream' of integration was lamented.[43] The Euro-dollar metaphor was widely used to imply a contest in which newcomers were checking American unilateralism politically and economically.[44]

---

[40]   Foreign Minister Ahmed Maher on the occasion of signing the partnership agreement, *Al-Ahram* editorial *Al-Ahram*, 26 June 2001; Raouf Saad, Egyptian Ambassador to the EU, *Al-Ahram*, 2 July 2001.

[41]   'Egyptian Industry gets ready for Competition: Experts confirm that Industrial Modernisation is a Must,' *Al-Ahram*, 2 July 2001; El Sayyed Elewa, 'The European Partnership and Strategic Choice,' *Al-Ahram*, 27 June 2001.

[42]   Gad, 'A Call for Contemplating the European Experience of Joint Action,' *Al-Ahram*, 20 April 2003. *Al-Ahram* Opinion, 'Another Lesson from Europe,' *Al-Ahram*, 1 December 2003; Abdel Aziz Hamouda, 'The European Union and the Arab Union,' *Al-Ahram*, 17 February 2004.

[43]   Mohamed Salmawi, 'The Euro and the Arab Dream of Unity,' *Al-Ahram*, 7/11/2001. 'The Euro: A Miracle and a Model,' *Al-Ahram*, 6 March 2002.

[44]   El Lawendi, 'The Euro: A Symbol for European Rebellion Against American Hegemony,' *Al-Ahram*, 12 December 2001.

95

The positive media representation of Europe in the economic sphere sidelines the problems of competition and trade liberalisation associated with the partnership. This can be understood in light of the preferences of the media professionals in Egypt. In the aforementioned opinion poll conducted by Al-Ahram Centre for Political and Strategic Studies in 2000,[45] media professionals welcomed the Euro-Mediterranean Partnership. In answer to a question on whether the EMP was the best framework for regional integration, twenty-eight per cent of media professionals thought it was the best, ranking second after business groups, who favoured the EMP with a larger majority of thirty-eight per cent, while only 12 per cent of the public agreed.

Compared to Arab regionalism, the EMP came out as the second-best alternative according to media professionals in terms of a positive potential impact on the Egyptian economy. Whereas almost half ranked Arab regionalism foremost among regional integration frameworks, only a sixth ranked the EMP first. Moreover, a quarter of respondents ranked Arab regionalism as the second-best for economic welfare, compared to sixteen per cent for the EMP. However, when asked which framework they considered more feasible and applicable, twenty-eight per cent of media professionals chose the EMP, compared with a quarter for Arab regionalism.

In this respect, the EMP seems to be the second most preferred alternative among media circles for regional integration, following Arab integration. The EMP's credibility as a viable alternative, however, exceeded that of Arab regionalism, which was ideologically and emotionally favoured.

Nevertheless, it is unclear whether this positive representation is irreversible. There are other factors to consider, such as the emerging responses towards the New Neighbourhood Initiative, the waning of the initial optimism about development through bilateral and regional economic cooperation, and finally

---

[45]   See Soltan *et al.*

with the potentially negative impact of trade liberalisation on vulnerable economic sectors. In these circumstances, the positive image of Europe in the economic sphere hinges upon the EU's ability to maintain the image of the exemplar and facilitator of development, in contrast to the image of the Leviathan, which is slowly gaining ground against the backdrop of enlargement. A case in point is the muted media response to the Union for the Mediterranean, as compared to the initial optimism regarding the EMP, despite positive official stances and the more recent leading role for Egypt in the initiative with the co-chairmanship of Egyptian President Hosni Mubarak.

Europe as pro-reform power?

Although there is a clear – if fluctuating – tendency to represent Europe as a political ally, there is no similarly positive definition of Europe as a power for political reform in the Egyptian media, whether official, opposition or independent. This can be attributed to a number of factors: firstly, Europe's new reform agenda for the Mediterranean has caused confusion among official circles in Egypt, who have been among the foremost promoters of partnership with Europe. Meanwhile, the public at large, and reform activists in particular, have not yet developed a strong commitment to the EU reform agenda, on the grounds of lack of resolve on both sides, as well as a lack of consistency or continuity in EU policies. Hence, the resulting representation of Europe as a power for political reform takes on a highly defensive tone, and the media are critical of foreign-promoted political reform.

One example is the German Foreign Minister's declaration on political reform in the Middle East at the Munich Security Conference in February 2004, which caused great confusion in the Egyptian public debate on Europe. The aftermath of the reform initiative saw the rise of anti-western sentiments in the media, especially the national media, which put the EU with the US in one patronising camp. Through historical references to the colonial era and even to the crusades, 'the West' was depicted as trying to manipulate the Arab world through false calls for reform. Commenting on the German Foreign Minister's initiative, prominent columnist Salah Eddin Hafez mocked the 'auction of democratic reform initiatives'.[46] Other editorials portrayed the initiative as part of a new guardianship and relapse to the colonial era.[47]

Hence, the credibility of the Europeans as partners hit its lowest point with accusations that EU member states were working to maximise their individual interests through the Greater Middle East Initiative, against the interests of the region.[48] Beyond its actual substance, the way in which the initiative was declared – without prior consultation – turned Europe in the media into a hegemon. This representation saw the EU grouped together with the US into one hostile camp, leading to the denunciation of the positive image of Europe as a 'grand delusion'.[49]

A less dominant line of argument in the media, however, sought to outline the differences between American and European approaches to Arab reform, and to point out areas of congruence between Egyptian and European positions. Meanwhile, another trend lamented the EU's inability to enforce its different views of reform, namely those which include emphasis on the unresolved Palestinian tragedy and on terrorism.[50]

Another case in point which illustrates the negative representation of Europe's reform agenda is that of the European Parliament's January 2008 resolution condemning Egypt's human rights record. The resolution caused widespread criticism from national and independent media alike. Most editorials emphasised the contrast between Europe's condemnations of human rights in

---

[46] Salah Eddin Hafez, 'Democratic Reform in the Euro Mediterranean Auction,' *Al-Ahram*, 18 February 2004.

[47] Salama, 'The Region Under Guardianship,' *Al-Ahram*, 19 February 2004.

[48] Abdel A'ati Mohamed, 'Non-reformist Initiatives,' *Al-Ahram*, 24 February 2004.

[49] El Lawendi, 'Europe: The Grand Delusion,' *Al-Ahram*, 25 February 2004.

[50] Gamal Badawi, 'The Middle East under Intensive Care,' *Al-Wafd*, 27 February 2004.

Egypt and the way it was ignoring the siege in Gaza that very month. The main criticism was one of hypocrisy, which saw Europe turn a blind eye to the status of human rights in Gaza while seeing fit to criticise Egypt.

The independent media's condemnation of the resolution only differed in terms of placing equal blame on the Egyptian regime's inability to check what was seen as Zionist influence on the European parliament.[51] Some independent media editorials drew a comparison with the cartoon crisis, condemning Europe's discourse on human rights at the time and its lack of respect for the religion of more than a billion Muslims.[52] A third trend condemned the regime's verbal rejection of European policies while quietly acquiescing to externally dictated policies. This trend warned against a future acknowledgement of same-sex marriage, and the besieging of Palestinians in Gaza in response to European pressures.[53] The dominant representation of Europe in reform matters here was one of hypocrisy and double standards. It is noteworthy, however, that independent media channels were the forum for some human rights activists, who, despite not refuting the overall trend of condemnation, described the Egyptian government's reaction as 'hysterical'.[54]

Europe as cultural hegemon?

Compared with political and economic dimensions, cultural representations of Europe have assumed the least importance in the Egyptian media debate. The general trend has been one of cultural neutrality. The debate on Egypt's Mediterranean identity may be century-old. However, only seldom if ever does it find its way into the media. Nevertheless, cultural representations of Europe have always been vulnerable to political developments. Negative

---

[51] Mahmoud Mussalam, 'The Media and the World,' *Al-Masry Al-Youm*, 18 March 2008.

[52] Osama Heikal, 'Rights for Sale,' *Al-Masry Al-Youm*, 15 March 2008.

[53] Mahmoud Khalil, 'Releasing Ayman Nour and Acknowledging Same Sex Marriage,' *Al-Masry Al-Youm*, 10 February 2008.

[54] Bahey Eddin Hassan, *Al-Masry Al-Youm*, 9 March 2008.

developments in the latter tend to spill over into temporarily negative cultural representations.

Prior to the Danish cartoon crisis, the scant media representation of European cultural issues in Egypt could be explained in light of the much greater importance of the economic aspects of the European partnership, and of Europe's political role in the Middle East. However, unspoken fears of cultural hegemony seem to have been concealed beneath the surface. The detailed *Al-Ahram* coverage of the official Egyptian response to EU positions on sexual equality and freedom[55] was indicative of considerable public support for the official stance. The latter was seen as protecting the local value system from 'foreign intrusions'. There was apprehension about the enforcement of 'universal rights' that might contradict cultural or religious heritage. The issues cited varied from the Islamic inheritance system, to the death penalty, to same-sex marriage. The apprehension here concerns not only what are envisioned as irreconcilable value differences per se, but also the top-down, patronising approach through which the EU declares its attitudes on cultural matters.[56]

Cultural aspects of representation started to gain further visibility at a moment of extreme political strain, namely with the beginning of the 'war on terror' discourse. This produced an increasingly polarised cultural representation of Europe, particularly in the new media. The four fronts on which the 'war on terror' were fought were Afghanistan, Iraq, Lebanon, and Palestine: all of the nations under attack were considered to be mostly Muslim.[57] Therefore, cultural assertiveness became increasingly prevalent, and

---

[55]   See *Al-Ahram*, 1 December 2001.

[56]   Sameh Abdallah and Magdi El Hosseini, 'Europe and Us: the beginning of a New Phase,' *Al-Ahram*, 4 February 2001.

[57]   Diaa Rashwan, 'Which model would the Catholic Church choose for conducting its relations with Muslims?,' *Cairo Commentary*, September 2006. http://acpss.ahram.org.eg/eng/ ahram /2004 /7/5/EGYP69.HTM

the cartoon incident came to pass in a highly charged cultural and political context.

The Danish Cartoon Crisis

The Danish cartoon crisis in September 2005 was a turning point in the cultural representation of Europe in the Egyptian media. The crisis dominated public debates across the world, with opinion leaders, politicians, intellectuals, clergymen and religious scholars all offering their views. Perceived by a majority in the Arab and Muslim world as an offence against symbols of religious belief, and by most in Europe as an instance of freedom of expression, cultural polarisation began assuming irreconcilable proportions.

It is noteworthy that the crisis was associated in Egypt with the private or independent media, since *Al-Fagr* ('The Dawn'), a weekly independent paper, initially published the cartoons in its print and online versions. Yet overall, the national, opposition and new media alike conveyed culturally polarised representations of Europe, although the cartoon coverage in the new media was more intensive. Following the lead of the Gulf media, which had brought up the issue earlier and called for a boycott, different Egyptian media channels, very limited exceptions aside, used a mobilising and confrontational discourse, as well as negative representations of Europe and the West.

Most newspapers criticised the European media, with the leading daily *Al-Gumhuriyya* ('The Republic') repeatedly calling the cartoons 'a conspiracy against Islam and Muslims which has been at work for years'. Yet again, the representation was of Europe's hypocrisy, as it was criticised for banning holocaust denial while allowing the defamation of sacred Islamic symbols. The cartoon/holocaust comparison was the benchmark of Europe's cultural representation in the Egyptian media.

Cultural representation during the cartoon crisis drew upon selective sources of information, including Danish and European opinion polls which consented to the publication of the cartoons,[58] while ignoring any moderate positions that would shake or refute this assertion of cultural polarisation. Europe was thus represented as Islamophobic, the home of the crusaders, and as waging war against Islam.

Religious sentiments, already flaring up over the occupation of Iraq, made matters worse. Many in the media portrayed the cartoons issue as part of a wider offensive against Islam, its sacred values, and its followers. As religion, politics, and history became entangled in this selective manner, a tone of hostility to the West evolved – one that cited the crusades and the ongoing conflicts in Iraq and Palestine in the same breath. Some media channels even drew comparisons between the military assault on Muslim countries and the cultural assault on the Muslim world.[59]

Satellite television channels played a prominent role during the cartoon crisis, although not consistently focusing on European matters. Most popular talk shows rallied the public around a package of hostile actions, of which economic boycott was perhaps the mildest. The Orbit Field Production unit (OFP), and its popular three-hour Arabic language show *Al-Qahira Al-Youm* ('Cairo Today'), was among the main mobilisers for an economic boycott.

Responding to the public outcry, and aiming at larger audiences and readership, private and independent media played the most visible role in mobilising public anger further. Acting purely in the manner of 'private business' according to some analysts, the private media played on public emotions and sacred symbols, to jump with circulation to unbound horizons',

---

[58] Khaled Salah, 'Between Religion, the State, and Capital, the Egyptian Media and the Cartoon Crisis,' Paper Presented to the Conference: Freedom of Expression Across Cultures, Cairo Institute for Human Rights Studies, December, 2006, p. 5. http://www.cihrs.org/Act_file/ PDF/ 85_111220064942.pdf

[59] *Ibid.*

thus producing a much more negative representation of Europe compared with that in the mainstream media.[60]

Only a year after the cartoon crisis had settled down, negative cultural representations returned in reaction to Pope Benedict XVI's controversial remarks on some of Islam's tenets and the actions of Prophet Muhammad, made during a lecture at the University of Regensburg in September 2006. The Pope's remarks became the focus of media attention and were portrayed as insulting. They reignited the cycle of mistrust, and the cultural representation of Europe as the 'West' in the negative sense. As the pope's lecture had been understood to suggest that Islam lacked reason and condoned violence, spreading by the sword rather than by persuasion, some media trends viewed the remarks as intended to justify the war on terror. By providing a Christian pretext for a politically-motivated war, Muslims felt that the Pope had taken sides.[61] In other words, cultural representations of Europe, while gaining more visibility, became more vulnerable to political sensitivities, which led to cultural polarisations and negative representations.

Conclusion

Europe is generally represented in the Egyptian media as a political ally and an economic partner. In addition, the European Union maintains the image of the exemplary model for Arab development and integration. This representation is more evident in the mainstream media, which pays more attention to Europe.

However, viewing Europe as a political ally hinges upon many contextual factors, the European role in the Arab-Israeli conflict and lately the war on

---

[60]   *Ibid.*
[61]   Rashwan, 'Which model', 2006.

Iraq being the most important. In this respect, failing to meet the expectations held of a political ally causes media criticism of the EU.

The cultural aspects of Europe's image have been less evident, and cultural issues pertaining to relations with European countries were rarely a matter of media focus until the cartoon crisis, before which Europe's media image was mostly culturally neutral. The cartoon crisis pushed to the surface anxieties about value differences which were previously held in check by the overall positive outlook towards Europe. The peak of the crisis was given the most momentum by satellite channels and talk shows. References were made to Europe's colonial past and some metaphors even went back to the crusades. However, negative representations of Europe during the crisis generally reflected disappointment at the war on terror and a feeling of being a target and powerless, rather than hostility to European values per se. The crisis subsided without making a long-term impact on the cultural image of Europe, despite setting a precedent for a cultural or religious matter of difference to assume that kind of centrality in the media debate on Europe in the future.

Overall, then, the cartoon crisis has brought more attention to Europe in the Egyptian media, but has left it with a less favourable image than before. Despite not having long-term repercussions for Europe's media representation, the incident may have ended what might be termed as the 'romantic' era of representations of Europe in the Egyptian media. The future of Europe's image will be contingent upon a number of factors, the first being the less confrontational American policy in the region expected from the coming administration. If the highest tide of positive representation was shaped in contrast to unwanted American policies, a less differentiated American policy in the region could detract from Europe's representation as the moral or just power. Second, the unforeseen emergence of sensitive cultural issues could also negatively affect Europe's media representation, although the recurrence of incidents which match the impact of the cartoon crisis is unlikely. This is further supported by the toned down reaction to the second publishing of the cartoons. Third, the development of new forms of the partnership, most recently the Union for the Mediterranean (UfM), have the potential to positively affect Europe's image in case of significant developments. However, so far this new framework has attracted less media coverage than the EMP, which might contradict the notion of official influence. Despite clear official interest in the new framework for cooperation, less media enthusiasm in terms of volume and tone of coverage has been reflected so far, the prevalent media stance being one of 'wait and see'. However, slow developments or reversals on the UfM might not only decrease representations of Europe's image further, but might even perpetuate the image of Europe as a power that does not deliver.

Chapter Five

Intimacy and contempt: the idea of Europe in the Turkish press

Andrew Finkel

In the recent brawling over the political mayhem in the Balkans, a dangerous prejudice masquerades as an analytic perspective. It is a prejudice far more deeply and more insidiously entrenched than the atavism it claims to have identified in Balkan society at large and that it cites as the pretext for condescension and hegemony. It is the view that pits the allegedly rational democracies of Western Europe against states whose European identity is itself at issue – states that are variously characterized as unstable, kinship based, and small scale. The irony of this perspective is of course that the language in which it is couched is itself that of kinship: that of the stern parent chastising a wayward and fractious brood of children.

Michael Herzfeld, *Cultural Intimacy*[1]

Recep Tayyip Erdoğan, the Turkish prime minister educated at a parochial Islamic high school, was once caught on camera as a youthful activist sitting at the feet of the proto-Taliban warlord Gulbeddin Hekmatyar. In 2004, the press battery of cameras captured Mr Erdoğan in a very different setting. He was seated in front of a vast bronze statue of Pope Innocent X in the Grand Hall of the Michelangelo inspired Campidoglio. The exact date was 29th October, and

---

[1]   Michael Herzfeld, *Cultural Intimacy: Social Poetics in the Nation-state* (London: Routledge, 2004) 2nd edition, p. 127.

one more normally commemorated in Turkey as the day on which the Republic was founded after the hard-fought release from Greek and Western European occupation at the end of the First World War. However, the Turkish premier was in Rome not to celebrate national sovereignty but to barter it away. Along with the new members of the recently enlarged European Union (EU), the soon to be admitted candidates Bulgaria and Romania, as well as Ankara's fellow EU hopeful Croatia, Turkey put its signature to the final declaration of the new, albeit ill-fated, European Constitution.

It was at a no less perfectly stage-managed photo opportunity that the then American president explained the significance of the historical process in which Turkey and Europe were engaged. George W. Bush was speaking at the 2004 NATO summit, the first meeting of the Western alliance since the invasion of Iraq, which was being held in Istanbul, the principal city of NATO's sole Muslim-majority member nation. The president delivered his open-air address at a university that bordered the Bosphorus Straits and against a backdrop rich in symbolism. Behind him was the very modernist bridge which links Europe to Asia, and in the middle distance was a nineteenth century neo-baroque mosque (designed, as it happens, by the father and son Armenian architects, Garabet and Nigogayos Balyan). Mr Bush cleared his throat to deliver a spirited defence of NATO's new mission to grapple with the asymmetric threat of terrorism, but underlying his remarks was an expression of dismay at the disrepute into which the values underpinning the alliance had fallen. At one point he even felt obliged to reassure his listeners in the Islamic world that 'there is nothing incompatible between democratic values and high standards of decency.'[2] However, the remark which made the headlines in the Turkish press, the BBC and on CNN was the implied rebuke to the French, already on bad terms with Washington for their opposition to the invasion of

---

[2] Full text in *The Guardian*, http://www.guardian.co.uk/world/2004/jun/29/eu.nato1

Iraq. The French president, Jacques Chirac, was assumed to be the most obdurate opponent to the EU's pending decision on whether to initiate accession negotiations with Turkey. On reflection, President Bush might have bitten his tongue, considering that the one thing that could well stand in the way of Europe accepting Turkish candidacy is for it to feel it should do so at the behest of the Americans.[3] Nonetheless, the symbolism of Turkish entry was too potent for the US president's speech writers to ignore: 'Including Turkey in the EU would prove that Europe is not the exclusive club of a single religion; it would expose the "clash of civilizations" as a passing myth of history,'[4] he said.

George Bush has not been the only one to define Turkey's relationship with Europe as a grand, epochal challenge – and to depict Mr Erdoğan's own 'Road to Brussels' conversion, along with Turkey's inclusion in the enlargement mechanism, as both an amulet and practical bulwark of Europe's defence. According to Joschka Fischer, the German former Green Party Vice Chancellor, 'To modernize an Islamic country based on the shared values of Europe would be almost a D-Day for Europe in the war against terror.'[5] And no less an authority than Osama bin Laden also recognised the unique position of Turkey in the Islamic world. In one of his post-9/11 video appearances, he explained that he was out to avenge 'eight decades of pain, humiliation and shame.' The reference, Turks grasped at once, was to the creation of their own republic in 1923 and to the decision of its founder, Mustafa Kemal Atatürk, to plough salt into the notion of a theocratic state.

---

[3] Jacques Chirac (also in Turkey for the only visit of his 12 year presidency) responded immediately by saying that the US president had 'ventured too far and into territory that is not his concern'.
See 'Chirac clashes with Bush over Turkey' at http://www.euractiv.com/ en/enlargement/chirac-clashes-bush-turkey/article-118074. In fact, Chirac did eventually support the opening of negotiations with Turkey in 2004 (against the wishes of his successor, then Interior Minister, Nicholas Sarkozy).
[4] See *The Guardian*, http://www.guardian.co.uk/world/2004/jun/29/eu.nato1
[5] Quoted in Chris Morris, *The New Turkey: the quiet revolution on the edge of Europe* (London: Granta Books, 2005), p. 197.

There were no photographers on hand to capture the lurid complexion of the British Foreign Secretary, Jack Straw, 'purple with concentration',[6] at the twelfth hour negotiations in Brussels on 3rd October 2005. That day, the formal start of negotiations between Turkey and the EU might have been expected to represent the ceremonial commemoration of an important milestone in more than four decades of Turkish efforts to ally itself with European institutions. Instead, it turned into a day and a long night of bitter Euro-haggling, memorable for the public reluctance of the Austrian foreign minister to turn the other cheek over the 1683 Ottoman siege of Vienna.[7] Less memorable, if only because it was less well publicised, was the EU's attempts to manoeuvre Ankara into removing its right of veto over Cypriot accession to NATO. The intrinsic pettiness of diplomatic horse-trading could not distract from the profundity of the moment, in which Turkey was very publicly engaged in a political process whose ultimate aim was to enter into a political union which would help it decide the future of some of the world's largest economies and most mature democracies. The Turkish press, like their European counterparts, had cleared the front pages for the occasion, and the headlines hailed the moment with the same sort of enthusiasm for Europe with which they had once greeted the collapse of the Berlin Wall. It was proof of Turkish perseverance, not just at implementing an accession agreement dating from 1963, but at 'a two-century quest to integrate with modern civilisation.'[8] These were the words of a prominent leader writer for the nationalist *Hürriyet* newspaper, better known for his suspicions of Western Europe's motives towards Turkey.

---

[6]   I quote here and in other obvious places in the text from my own reporter's notepad.

[7]   Curiously enough, Turks themselves have learned to deal with this particular part of history with irony. When the Turkish press speaks of the 'siege of Vienna', it is normally a cliché reference to a football match between a Turkish and an Austrian side.

[8]   Otkay Ekşi, 'Üç kavga bizi bekliyor' ('three disputes await us'), *Hürriyet* newspaper, 5 October 2005.

However, the civilisation to which the *Hürriyet* writer was referring was not Samuel Huntington's Judeo-Christian monolith, with its structural tendency to clash with a Turkish culture rooted in Islam. Rather (and I extrapolate), it was a post-French revolutionary civilisation based on rationalism, and one which had inspired the founders of the Turkish Republic. It was, moreover, a civilisation from which Europe itself was prone to stray.[9] Just as the old Rome (to extrapolate further) had moved to Constantinople to escape barbarism in the fourth century, so too a Turkish secular elite continued to safeguard European rationalism for a Europe which had become too stale and hypocritical to do the job itself. *Hürriyet*, apart from being Turkey's most profitable newspaper, is also the house organ of the Turkish establishment. Its front page motto translates 'Turkey belongs to the Turks' and the readership to which it caters bristles in outrage at the notion that Western governments identify Turkey as a moderate Islamic nation that serves as a model for the region. They relegated Islam long ago to the status of hand-servant to Turkish nationalism, and rebel at the thought that more public space might be available to a trans-national Islam outside their control. True to form, the commentator was one of many who saw the launch of negotiations not as a downhill ride, but as the start of a process of pre-programmed crises, as Europe called upon Turkey to make concessions which would be perceived as contradicting its national interest. The squabbles over Cyprus were just one bump in the road ahead, one which would be demarcated not simply with milestones of reform but with political landmines and threats to established elites.

---

[9] The idea that the Turkish Republic has become the doomsday vault for European values and a Europe condemned to destroy itself was a prevalent one in Turkey at the end of the First World War. For a contemporary description see Demetra Vaka Brown, *The Unveiled Ladies of Istanbul* reprinted from the 1923 edition (New Jersey: Gorgias Press, 2005).

If the Turkish media's perception of Europe is more complex, volatile or ambivalent than many other Muslim majority nations, it is because the fate of the country whose opinions it reflects is inextricably intertwined with Europe's own. This was the case before officials from Ankara and Brussels sat down to negotiate shared sovereignty. The number of those of Turkish origin living in Europe exceeds 5 million – roughly the population of Denmark. At an equally basic level, Turkey and Europe have had a customs union of manufactured goods since 1995, the first step in a commitment to complete Turkish integration made in 1963 by the Ankara Agreement. As a result Turkey applies an external tariff regime decided in Brussels, and conducts the majority of its own trade with EU member states. Up until the current economic crisis, European direct and indirect investment had been pouring into a country which happens to be its fifth largest export market. At last glance, Turkey ranked as the fifteenth largest world economy, and those in favour of Turkish entry are eager to stress the win-win situation of incorporating a relatively virgin market for goods and financial services contiguous to Europe's existing boundaries. Even those unenthusiastic about Turkey's inclusion calculate the consequences of confessing this to Ankara's face and of allowing the country to drift outside the European orbit. While some member states openly question Turkey's 'Europeanness', they still do not have the courage of their lack of conviction to allow negotiations to collapse. 'Tens of thousands of jobs in the EU depend on economic growth in Turkey, while job creation in Turkey depends also on the fast growing interdependence with the EU economy,' is the gloss painted by Günter Verheugen, European commissioner for trade and industry.[10]

Of course interdependence can sometimes breed contempt, and the issues which loom largest in Turkey's laborious accession to full EU membership are

[10]   Günter Verheugen, 'Turkey belongs to Europe', speech in Ankara, 19 January 2007.

not necessarily the sub-clauses of environmental protocols, nor the misperception which Turks have of the European institutions they aspire to join, but rather the public ordeal of conforming to criteria of adequacy in order to be accepted as European. In Turkish eyes, this is interpreted as submitting to a detailed and at times humiliating judgment of every aspect of its society, from the behaviour of its judges and gaolers to the quality of its effluent.

There is, of course, a liberal body of public opinion in Turkey eager to see the nation run this gauntlet of reform and similarly eager to enlist an external authority to add weight to their own criticisms of their society. The (minority) overtly liberal political press echoes European incomprehension at the failure of Turkish governments to repeal article 301 of the country's penal code, which infamously makes it an offence to 'insult Turkishness', and which has been used to persecute if not prosecute outspoken public figures. Yet even the majority conservative, nationalist press employ what Michael Herzfeld calls 'cultural intimacy',[11] an oddly reassuring sense of self-ridicule or self-irony which is used to create shibboleths and to demarcate identity. When a pedestrian falls into a negligently open manhole or an MP is suspected of having an illegal but religiously sanctioned second wife, the journalistic reflex is to ask how Turkey can possibly think it deserves to get into Europe. The press conducts the inverse sort of exercise when it registers its indignation at a 'fictive' Europe, whose intention is to divide Turkey and keep it weak, or when it complains that being the West's Muslim poodle is not the compliment they seek. Though the idea may be broadcast on national television or declared

---

[11] 'The recognition of those aspects of a cultural identity that are considered a source of external embarrassment but that nevertheless provide insiders with their assurance of common sociality, the familiarity with the bases of power that may at one moment assure the disenfranchised a degree of creative irreverence and at the next moment reinforce the effectiveness of intimidation.' See Herzfeld, *Cultural Intimacy*, p. 3.

across the front page of a daily newspaper, this is a private conversation, in a language Europeans are not meant to eavesdrop upon or understand.

By contrast, in order to press on with the EU entry agenda, governments feel obliged to nationalise the rhetoric of reform. With oratorical flourish, Tayyip Erdoğan re-labelled the Copenhagen Criteria for membership as the 'Ankara Criteria' – i.e. presenting them not as an alien imposition but as in line with what Turkey wishes for itself. This is an exercise in which Europe is happy to acquiesce. It parallels the European Commission's view of itself and of its procedures, namely that negotiations are conducted according to a moral paradigm which owes more to codes of chivalry than realpolitik and deals about Cyprus. States prove their worthiness through a commitment to protect the rights and prosperity of their people by adopting EU rules. Negotiations are about the pace but not the content of the transformation. The EU speaks confidently of the accession process as one of 'voluntary regime change' in which aspiring nations are not so much admitted to a club as corralled by a carefully crafted 80,000 page rule book of acquis communautaire.[12]

This is not the view expressed in the mainstream Turkish media. As far as they are concerned, Europe has one set of rules for Christian Europe and another for Turkey. Euroscepticism in Turkey does not mean distrust of European institutions as much as an inner conviction that no matter what Europe preaches, in practice, it cannot accept Turkey as an equal. Thus when Europe does exhibit fairness or pro-Turkish bias – such as initiating membership negotiations – this is lapped up in large headlines as diplomatic examples of 'man bites dog'. The Turkish press is rarely as simplistic as to depict Europe as 'polluting' or 'Satanic'. To be anti-European on principle neither wins votes in

---

[12] In the words of Olli Rehn, Member of the European Commission responsible for Enlargement, 'The accession negotiations are about determining how and when Turkey will adopt the EU acquis; the process is not on whether Turkey will adopt it. Each and every country, large or small, must meet the criteria to the letter. There are no shortcuts to Europe, only the regular route.' Speech, 'Accession negotiations with Turkey: fulfilling the criteria', delivered at the European Economic and Social Committee EU-Turkey Joint Consultative Committee, Brussels, 28 November 2005.

Turkey nor sells newspapers. The problematic is not Europe's otherness but its all too familiar hypocrisy. The more common perception in Turkey is that Europe has itself veered from its own ideals and that the process which it has used to engineer its own enlargement does not operate with any degree of justice. This observation is based in many cases on the experience of Turkish immigrant communities in Europe whose alienation was a current that fed into the Islamist politics of the 1970s. To Turkish secularists as well, the attempt by the German government to fob Ankara off with some formulaic 'privileged partnership', or that by the French to offer membership of a Mediterranean Union, is nothing more than assigning Ankara a permanent Gastarbeiter status. By contrast, when a German of Turkish origin becomes co-leader of the Green Party, the Turkish press hails this as an Obama-style triumph over European racism.

It might seem counterintuitive that even the 'religious' press rarely express offence at Europe, nor are fundamentally opposed to an alien system of values. There are exceptions to this rule: an openly Islamist newspaper called *Akit*, along with *Milli Gazete*, the party organ of the now disbanded Welfare Party, did print stories in the l990s which were the mirror images of the anti-EU diatribes of the nationalistic right in Europe. Such articles depicted Europe as a direct threat to Islamic practice, and the EU as a faceless bureaucracy intent on imposing standards that would undermine the values of nationhood. Europe, according to this minority voice, would stealthily impose – just as it had already done on the Turkish diaspora in Germany – regulations which would force Muslims to eat pork, prevent them from praying five times a day, or oblige Muslim women to behave immodestly. Yet even *Akit*, (rebranded *Vakit*) tempered this stance after it lent its support to the Justice and Development (AK) Party.

It is the AK Party which famously rewrote the political rulebook when it came to power in 2002, the last in a succession of parties descended from a more overtly Islamic movement. It was an openly reformist movement and a bold attempt to capture the political centre in the wake of an economic crisis which had decimated the more secular right-wing parties. The AK Party advertised themselves as committed to the free market, pro-European and pro-NATO, as well as far more capable of keeping Turkey's commitments to the IMF or the EU, all precisely because they were Nixons in China, able to command the allegiance of an 'authentic' Turkey, for they too had started out from a position of mistrust. It is clear that Europe, along with international business, were impressed by the first AK Party government (2002-2007), who focused on kick-starting EU membership negotiations and maintaining the tight fiscal discipline demanded by Turkey's anti-inflationary programme. However, to the AK Party's opponents, a traditional establishment which includes the military, it was this ability to win international acceptance which caused so much resentment and suspicion. In European eyes, the recognition given to the AK Party might have been no less than that given to any other democratically elected government. However, even this degree of legitimation was resented by that segment of Turkish society which regarded itself as the gatekeepers to modernity and the West. They felt that their role had been usurped and were looking for reasons for Europe's betrayal. The reasons became clearer when MEPs and other politicians spoke in defence of Kurdish rights, or lobbied for the recognition of the fate of the Armenian population in 1915 as genocide. Europeans, Turkish nationalists argued, were trying to achieve by crafty diplomacy the work they had begun with the First World War, that of fatally undermining the integrity of the nation.

There is a powerful anti-globalisation lobby inside Turkey, alongside a sector which sees Europe as a threat to their own power and influence. At the same time, it is a relatively safe generalisation that no public body wishes to be held accountable for the breakdown of negotiations, nor to appear to be against Europe. Curiously enough, this includes those now standing trial for attempting to bring about a coup d'état through violent acts of provocation – an event which, had it succeeded, would have extinguished Turkey's hopes of ever becoming politically integrated into the EU. The present author interviewed several defendants in what is popularly known as the 'Ergenekon conspiracy', including a retired colonel, Fikri Karadağ, who led a para-military group called *Kuvayi Milli*. In an on-the-record conversation, he declared himself entirely in favour of Turkish membership, but said that he was not foolish enough to think that Europe would ever commit itself to letting Ankara through the door. Europe's principal motive for conducting negotiations, he said, was to string Turkey along and induce her to enact what on the surface appeared to be reforms, but which in practice would weaken the 'backbone' of the nation.

Perhaps one source of misunderstanding between the EU and Turkey is that (with the exception of Sweden, which was also neutral during the Second World War), they are fighting different battles. It is, of course, the First World War and its aftermath which looms largest in Turkish memory. The rhetorical conflict Turkey has with the Armenian diaspora, the real skirmishes it has with Kurdish separatists, an obsession with Kirkuk, and the very independence the Republic celebrates against Greek and Allied occupation are all legacies of a confrontation which the rest of Europe has forgotten. Thus it comes as an incomprehensible surprise that there are elements in Turkey still prepared to re-enact the aftermath of the First World War over and over again.

The quotation at the beginning of this essay is Michael Herzfeld's anthropological assessment of another country's relationship to 'core' Europe, in this case Greece, where there are conflicting identities which interfere with Hellenic claims to being truly European. The official rhetoric of Greece as the birthplace of democracy and the home of Olympic ideals of noble (and free) competition conceals a much wilder notion of the 'true' Greece, where revelers toss plates into the fireplace and businessmen claim subsidies illegally. The contrast is similar in style if not precise content to that used by core member states of Europe to describe other candidates for enlargement, particularly those in what were once Ottoman domains. For Greece, becoming part of the EU meant reconnecting with Europe after the centuries of the Turkish night. Poland and Hungary were among the nations of Central and Eastern Europe welcomed back into the fold not after Ottoman, but Soviet occupation. The collapse of the Berlin Wall was the potent symbol of the end of a forced and unnatural separation. The image evoked by European enlargement is not that of an expansion of frontiers into dark unknown terrain, but rather that of a comfortable corpulence of middle age, a natural swelling after the anorexic anxiety of the Cold War.

However, if 'new Europe' is the discovery of natural boundaries after an era of artificial separation, then the identity of 'old Europe' was forged by the experiences of fascism, Bolshevism and European Wars. It was not all that long ago that the 'clash of civilisations' had nothing to do with the West and Islam but rather referred to the threat of Nazism. The pacification of Germany is a project very much at the cornerstone of the European project, and it is Germany which had to overcome both demons – fascism after 1945 and communism after 1989. The quotation from Joschka Fischer above is remarkable not just for his positing Turkish membership as the litmus test of European values, but for the way he equates this moral victory with D-Day, the Normandy invasion of the Third Reich. By contrast, Austria – one of the key advocates of standing against 'non-European' Turkey – was not only on the Axis side, but on the receiving end of diplomatic sanctions from its own EU partners, out of disapproval for a government that included the ultra-right Freedom Party.

Thus at the rhetorical level, succession candidates are not so much admitted, as welcomed back to Europe. Moreover, they are admitted through a purging of their past. The historical cleavages between Protestant and Catholic or Catholic and Orthodox fade into insignificance in a Europe which has managed to overcome the post-war chasm between France and Germany, and where Spain and Greece were rewarded for discarding their dictatorships. The German Greens may wish to see Europe atone by admitting Turkey and indeed elect Cem Özdemir, the son of a Gastarbeiter, to jointly lead the party. Yet theirs is not the only voice. To many in Europe, to negotiate with Turkey is to engage in a process which can offer no catharsis. It is at best a practical decision to expand the European market, and at worst an attempt to impose discipline on a potentially unstable neighbour. European conservatives – those with whom the AK Party might be expected to have a natural affinity – are the most active in keeping Turkey at arm's length. Thus when Cardinal Ratzinger, the current Pope, appeared, he lobbied for the Christian character of Europe to be enshrined in its constitution. The inescapable logic of this move was to deny Turkey the possibility of redemption through accession. There is, to take a parallel example, a similarly pointed refusal by the European press to understand honour killings as an all too recognisable manifestation of the sort of domestic violence which abounds in most European cities – and therefore explainable through an analysis not of cultural determinism but of social change. Instead, it is depicted as a dark, atavistic phenomenon stubbornly rooted in the very alien character of Islamic or even pre-Islamic societies. To be fair, the European press is no different from Turkey's own Istanbul-centred media, who depict crimes of honour as Eastern or Kurdish phenomena which they cannot understand.

One could argue that the historical reality is very different from these depictions, and that if there is such a thing as a unitary history of Europe, then

Turkey and the Ottoman Empire form a part of that history. Conflict within Christian Europe was far more intense than conflicts between Christians and Muslims, Turks may argue, despite their persistence well into the nineteenth century when Western powers intervened in the Ottoman controlled Holy Lands, with language grounded in the Crusades. Yet Turkish nationalists and European exclusionists remember a history of incompatibility.

Consequently, those who seek to extol the virtues of Turkey's EU application do so by arguing the need for Europe to address its own fear. Why should an enlargement process which worked for a staggering array of entrants, from Portugal to Bulgaria, simply break down in the case of Turkey? Yet sections of European public opinion – with fears based initially on the challenge of assimilating their own immigrant populations, and for nearly a decade on a fear of Islamic-inspired militancy – view Turkish accession much in the way it would a boa constrictor and the cow it is about to consume. They wonder if this might not be the unique case of a country which is as able to choke EU institutions as it is to be absorbed by them. A country like Britain, buoyed by the editorial writers of its quality press, has consistently advocated Turkish entry. Yet even here there is a suspicion that British support (prior to the collapse of the Lisbon Treaty) was also founded on the hope that Turkey's accession would be the final requiem for a federal Europe.

That the road to EU membership has been far rockier for Turkey than other candidates is, therefore, not so much a 'misunderstanding' as the elephant in the room. Turks accuse Europe of hypocrisy, arguing that their candidacy is hopelessly stalled, and subject to European ill-will and prejudice masquerading as bureaucratic officiousness and red tape. However, liberal opinion in Turkey also accuses its own government of dragging its feet. This view is fuelled by the suspicion that the government aspires more to the medium term benefits which actual candidacy can bring (such as higher levels of foreign direct investment) and wishes to minimise the political cost of enacting painful reforms. Unsurprisingly, EU entry now seems a far-off Shangri-La, and a political project from which ordinary readers are increasingly disengaged. A series of self-defence mechanisms have kicked in, alongside a degree of pragmatism. Now is not the time to risk humiliation by being seen to want EU admission, but rather to wait in the wilderness until a new generation of more sympathetic European leaders comes to power.

***

'All politics is local', was the memorable watchword of Tip O'Neill, the hard-nosed Speaker of the US House of Representatives of the 1970s and 1980s. One assumes that a politician reared during the New Deal, when party machines handed out turkeys at Christmas, meant nothing more Delphic by this than that voters judged the great issues of the day through an optic of immediate experience. However as an axiom for public life, it at least avoids the 'it's the economy stupid' arbitrage of big ideas to the coinage of self-interest. It is intriguing because it expresses, in the brass tacks language of boss politics, a complex metaphor of power as a question of social distance. When power becomes too attenuated, it fades. This is a reminder that Europe as a political idea only makes sense if it is anchored in domestic politics. In this, the role of the press is central.

A plausible view of recent Turkish politics has been that of a tense struggle between two rival elites. The first is grounded in the ideology of the Kemalist revolution and sees progress and development as emanating from a centre – a zone of legitimate power to which entry is meritocratic, and which involves passing through a series of finely meshed cultural filters. One such screen tests for an ability to deal instrumentally with rival claims to legitimation, be they Islam or Europeanism, should they conflict with the core commitment to the nation-state. The second elite is motivated by a form of Islamic Calvinism that offers economic success as proof of piety. It associates freedom of religious observance with that of economic association as the real point of democracy and political activism. Above all, it nurtures a sense of grievance at being made to feel inferior by the first elite.

It is scarcely contentious to argue that the media is not a window pane through which its consumers view events, but rather a distorting optic which helps individuals construct a complex view of themselves through a series of overlapping identities of family, community, football club, religion and nation as well as of supra-national Europe. Such powerful allegiances and bonds to often abstract institutions can come at the expense of what might appear to be immediate self-interest. The reification of the state, and the precedence of ties forged by nationalism over the solidarity of economic class, once posed a knotty problem to classical Marxist analysis. It was this issue which Benedict Anderson addressed in his classic study of nationalism, in which he stressed the centrality of a print-language to the historical process of constructing his eponymous 'imagined community', a (political) construct outside the realm of immediate experience with which individuals nonetheless identify.[13] Similarly, one can see the centrality of print and televised images as key tools not just in creating, but also in controlling abstract loyalties. The media does not simply allow individuals to expand their horizons, it also sets the frontiers of these horizons.

The issue is complicated further because the Turkish press, not unlike many other national media, is itself Janus-faced. It seeks legitimacy as the Fourth Estate committed to transparency, but also shows its hand as a political actor at times, attempting to fill the public realm with static rather than open debate. Its partisanship is motivated by a concept of the national good and by

---

[13] Benedict Anderson, *Imagined Communities: Reflections on the Origin and Spread of Nationalism* (London: Verso, 1955), p. 44ff.

political ideology at times, and at others by the more tangible pecuniary concerns of its proprietors, who reap rent through access to state decision making in non-press sectors. The media barters its influence over and access to politicians through an ability to set the national news agenda. If Turkish domestic politics is deeply polarised, the press is instrumental in this.

To take a series of conflicting examples: among those indicted in the Ergenekon trial are journalists accused of seeking to manipulate public opinion in order to prepare the way for a military coup. Similarly, the Turkish press resounds with accusations that the Ergenekon trial itself is an attempt by the government to intimidate its opponents, and in particular, those who supported the attempts by the Constitutional Court's proceedings in 2008 to shut down the AK Party. Europe (to take a quite different set of examples) is sometimes presented as an antidote to Turkey's Kurdish problem, i.e. a supranational framework to resolve a regional dispute. The argument is not just that Turkey will make concessions to cultural minority rights under EU pressure, but also that the prospect of EU membership would give the Kurds an incentive to strengthen a civic commitment which contains a passport to a European identity. Yet the Turkish press also presents Europe as an agitator for Kurdish autonomy, and even a promoter of separatist terror. The European press is depicted as concerned for Kurdish rights but oblivious to the victims of Kurdistan Workers Party (PKK) violence.

At the same time, the Turkish press can end polarisation, and deal playfully with misconceptions in much the same way as the British press parodies the way in which the rest of the world regards them as a Neverland of Sherlock Holmes eccentrics or PG Wodehouse aristocracy. This requires confidence. It is perhaps on the sports pages that the Turkish press feels most able to deal with Europe on a platform of equality, given that Turkish sportsmen have been more successful than their politicians. When sports writers speak of 'the siege of Vienna', they are referring to a Turkish team off to play FK Austria Wien.

To speak then, as this volume does, of mutual misunderstandings might at first be assumed to refer to the stuff of classical anthropology – the curious fact that different societies can give such diverse meanings to the same event or biological ritual. However, in the case of the press, these misunderstanding can be deliberate constructs and the result of huge expenditures and the investment of numerous man-hours by often creative and highly trained professionals. Europe has become a key cipher through which domestic wrangles and historic shifts in the balance of elite power are played out. The idea of Europe is dual edged – it represents a form of legitimacy for Turkey's historic mission and ultimate identity, but at the same time it represents a threat to sovereignty and an established order. Little wonder, then, in the deeply divided world of Turkish politics, that there is also a fight for control over the idea of Europe.

Little wonder too, perhaps, that Europe finds Turkey both daunting to include and too important to keep at arm's length. If Europe embraces Turkey, it will be to come to terms with its own identity and to lay to rest the idea of a Europe that defines itself by whom it can exclude rather than whom it can embrace. However, to many in Ankara, 'the clash of civilisations' is no passing myth, but a reality, and one taking place at home.

Chapter Six

Europe and Islam in Context, Identity *in* Politics: Concluding Remarks

Reem Abou-El-Fadl

> Much post-colonial theory shifted the focus from class and nation to ethnicity. This meant... that the distinctive problems of post-colonial culture were often falsely assimilated to the very different question of Western 'identity politics'. Since ethnicity is largely a cultural affair, this shift of focus was also one from politics to culture.

Terry Eagleton, *After Theory*[1]

The contributors to this volume have taken the media as their vantage point for an analysis of Self/Other representations across the purported European-Muslim divide. In five case studies from three continents, the contributors have reflected on the impact of the media's origins and development on these representations. As a result, the term 'media' has been unpacked to reveal a diversity of trends and counter-trends, public and private actors, traditional media, such as print, radio and television, and more recent forms such as satellite television and internet websites. Even the notion of 'mainstream' media has emerged as differentiated: such outlets cannot be divided easily into government or opposition mouthpieces, with either nationalist or liberal stances. In this sense, the media reflect the complexity of the wider debate on Europe and Islam, and the way the contributors have presented the media is primarily as a source for understanding this. They approach the media as a

---

[1]   Terry Eagleton, *After Theory* (London: Penguin Books, 2004), p. 12.

methodological tool through which to analyse processes of European integration and multiculturalism, international migration and North-South relations. Accordingly, we will focus here on approaches to the broader debates concerning Europe and Islam, with the media as a lens into them, rather than on the media *per se*.

In presenting the media as an illustration of each country's unique experience, the authors have pointed to the difficulties we face when dealing with such diversity. When comparing empirical cases, they have avoided reductionist categories. Indeed, the contributions in this volume have led us to question the idea of *mutual* misunderstandings itself – such terms might imply a sort of dichotomy which is reminiscent of the 'clash of civilisations' thesis, and might thus seem to endorse its cultural essentialism. In fact, the case studies have painted a very different picture, with accounts of the diversity within, and the intimacy between the so-called 'European' and 'Islamic worlds'.

On the other hand, while it is important to acknowledge diversity, it is equally necessary to be able to infer certain patterns for analysis. If there are various competing discourses, in different institutional and social contexts, what determines these discourses and how can we make sense of these differences? We will revisit our volume's contribution on this question via a brief look at alternative approaches in the literature.

The (a)politics of culture

Much of the literature on the 'Islam and Europe' debate chooses to foreground culture as an analytical category. The first example to consider is the 'clash of civilisations' view, which posits the 'European' and 'Muslim worlds' as self-contained cultures in an irremediable confrontation. This forms part of a larger *Weltanschauung* in which conflicts and alliances are determined by affinities or distance between 'cultural groups'. Academically, this view has been supported, among others, by Bernard Lewis and Samuel Huntington; empirically, it is maintained mainly by Islamophobes and certain Islamists, as our Introduction pointed out. Yet in this volume, where the authors acknowledge the existence of any 'clash', it is in the *political* field, whether over immigration policy, European accession or foreign relations. Meanwhile, where the authors and workshop participants debunk notions of a consistent clash, it is in the field of *culture*, for example in the Egyptian media's distinction between European politics and culture, or in the antiracism initiatives of 1980s Britain. The notion of inevitable clashes between cultural aggregates is therefore exposed as inaccurate and misleading. Indeed, the terms 'European' and 'Muslim-majority' are in themselves inadequate: the five case studies here might be more accurately described as two European Union countries with minority Muslim populations, two Muslim-majority countries, and one European country with a large Muslim community, all with secular states.

The second strand in the literature to consider comes often, though not always, from the postmodernist vein of cultural studies. Some of the scholarship on questions of multiculturalism and integration has sought to 'celebrate difference' with a focus on cultural discourses, particularly those of marginal or minority cultures. On the one hand, analysing such discourses can 'decentre' unhelpful binary oppositions of self/Other as Muslim/European to progressive effect. On the other hand, accounts which focus on a discursive analysis of culture can commit a dual error: firstly they may overlook the political, social and economic dimensions that determine what form a particular identity or boundary takes. Secondly, they may therefore gravely misrepresent the latter as simply discursive constructions that can be manipulated or deconstructed according to different needs. This notion is particularly unhelpful when it mirrors the narrative strategies of the political actors we are trying to analyse. Deltombe gives an example from France, where an elite 'has shifted the focus from genuine economic, social and political questions to a discriminatory focus on cultural and identity issues.' His response, and that of the authors in the volume, has been to highlight the interaction between socioeconomic factors and institutional structures on the one hand, and cultural expression on the other, and to look at the outcome in the *political* field.[2]

A key theme in this volume, then, and the key theme of this conclusion, is the limitations of focusing on culture – Islamic culture for example – as an analytical category, to the exclusion of other factors:

> To explain behaviour in terms of cultural values is to engage in circular reasoning. The assumption of inertia, that cultural and social continuity do not require explanation... [overlooks] the concrete interests and privileges that are served by indoctrination, education, and the entire complicated process of transmitting culture from one generation to the next.[3]

While all five authors have analysed discourses of culture in the media, they have highlighted the primacy of *politics* in shaping these, and the political field as their context. More specifically, the contributors emphasise that cultural discourses, such as those of nationalists in Europe or Muslim migrants, are informed by material factors. These include the socioeconomic status of migrants, institutions of education and social security, or the political power of governments for example. It is through their politicisation that culture and religion become relevant to debates on integration or citizenship today, and it is in connection with material power that certain discourses on culture become hegemonic. With this emphasis on politics, the contributors have provided us

---

[2] See Sami Zubaida, *Islam, the People and the State* (London: Routledge, 1989).

[3] Barrington Moore Jnr, *The Social Origins of Dictatorship and Democracy* (London: Allen Lane, 1967), p. 486.

with a means of tracking and comparing the diverse trends in self/Other representations in the five cases.

Ultimately, this leads us to question the use and juxtaposition of such simplistic categories as 'European' and 'Muslim' in our analyses, and to search for alternatives. It seems better to offer them as empirical examples of more generic analytical categories of 'identity' and 'Other'. It is better still to present these in a socioeconomic and political context that foregrounds the impact of material power and class on patterns of cultural belonging. For a millionaire oil sheikh from the Gulf likely has a lot more in common with the financial elites of Europe's capitals than with the Pakistani immigrant in Bradford. The two Muslims' views on democracy are probably radically different, and their abilities to realise them more different still. A German single mother might have a lot more in common with a peasant in Egypt than with her fellow nationals doing business in Dubai. The peasant may or may not be wearing a headscarf but will face depressingly similar challenges on bread and butter issues. In short, only a sound critique of culturalist arguments can enable us to locate Islamophobia and notions of East and West within their correct socioeconomic and *political* contexts.

The View from (Western) 'Europe'

The three accounts of media depictions of Islam in Western Europe, two in this volume, and one from the workshop on the UK case, have all pointed to the Islamophobia evident in these countries' political fields today. The authors speak of a political swing to the right in the 1980s that saw Muslims become the latest targets of intolerance in the three countries. This was reflected in the Honeyford Affair of the Thatcher years in Britain, the rise of the National Front in France, and of the conservative governments in post-unification Germany. The authors offer common explanations relating to the drying up of the need for (mostly Muslim) migrant labour by the 1970s with the onset of economic recession, and the host populations' failure to provide welfare and integration mechanisms for those 'guest workers' who wished to remain where they were.

From the authors' accounts, the theme that emerges is a gradual 'racialisation' of the Muslim religious group over recent decades. That is, Muslim has been transformed into a race-like category, through the description and often stigmatisation as 'Muslims' of many whose many other identity markers are overlooked. In the workshop and volume respectively, Samad and Deltombe have tracked the introduction of the new category of 'Muslim' into the public sphere by considering its use in the media. They assert its prevalence from the 1990s on, in media debates on a range of matters from civil strife to international relations, which reflect political discourses both on the right and left in Britain and France. Alternative ways of describing the diverse Muslim populations of these countries seem not to have gained wider currency. Samad and Deltombe also note Muslims' sub-classification in media and political discourses into 'moderate' or 'radical'. As Deltombe points out, the recent origins of this in the Bush doctrine of 'the war on terror'[4] mean that French journalists can speak of the social responsibilities of 'the Muslim community' in France after the 2001 attacks in the US. This has placed great strain on intercommunal relations. Although Samad acknowledges that many Muslims choose to self-identify as such in various spheres, both Samad and Deltombe place the emphasis on British and French politicians as spearheading their recent stigmatisation 'as Muslims', citing UK Home Office reports and the laws prompting the 'veil row' in France.

On the other hand, the contributors depict much European mainstream discourse and government policy on Muslims today as characteristic of an (Orientalist) prejudice with deep historical roots. This has simply been

---

[4]   See Mahmood Mamdani, *Good Muslim, Bad Muslim: America, the Cold War and the Roots of Terror* (New York: Pantheon, 2004).

updated from its colonial – or, according to Hafez, even medieval – context, right up to the contemporary 'war on terror' framework, in which it fulfils almost identical functions of inclusion/exclusion, and produces the same tropes of self/Other. The recent use of the 'us or them' language with regard to Muslims is indeed the latest manifestation of older frames of reference for such assorted 'Others' as the communist menace, the blacks, the Irish, and, before them, colonial subjects across Europe's colonies. The passing of formal empire gave way to the Cold War, which in turn gave way to the 'age of terror', and yet Western European elites' Others in each era have been represented in a remarkably consistent discourse. Each time, it has bemoaned a vaguely defined 'moral panic',[5] which condemned similarly vaguely defined 'folk devils'[6] at home, and their fearsome counterparts abroad.

In his workshop presentation, Samad traced the historical development of racist discourses in Britain from their targeting of visible difference, towards a subtler 'cultural' discrimination – from targeting blacks and Asians as different in colour or ethnicity, to targeting them as Muslims. In the French case, Deltombe points to the consistency between justifications for colonial and for Islamophobic prejudice. European colonialism was notorious for masking the ethnocentric nationalism of its *mission civilisatrice* with enlightenment values. Similarly, today's "conservative turn... wears the rhetorical mask of 'progress', 'modernity' and 'emancipation' – all concepts inherited from the 1789 Revolution..." This is ironically possible because in our postcolonial times, ethnocentric nationalism is concealed beneath the veil of laïcité, racialising Muslims while appearing to uphold the legitimate secular foundations of the republic.

---

[5]   This occurs when '[a] condition, episode, person or group of persons emerges to become defined as a threat to social values and interests.' Stanley Cohen, *Folk Devils and Moral Panics* (London: Routledge, 2002), p. 9.

[6]   *Ibid.*

Samad and Deltombe's discussions of Islamophobia remind us of the historically contingent nature of such political discourses. This historical perspective exposes the poverty of 'Islamic' or 'European culture' as explanatory terms. This is because historical precedents enlighten us as to when this or that religion was *not* necessarily central to relations between migrants and host populations, to integration efforts across a continent, or to foreign relations across two continents for example. Parallels might instead be drawn with other fraught relationships in history such as those between colonisers and colonised peoples, superpowers and middle range powers, or developed and developing nations. Thus through a historical perspective, we have seen how European security narratives have merely replaced race with religion as the latest manifestation of a far older pattern of discrimination.[7]

The Western European case studies also illustrate how contemporary political prejudices have been expressed in structural as well as discursive terms. Thus state elites might enmesh their narratives on national security with those on national identity, but these are realised through anti-terror legislation, tough immigration policies and military involvements in the Middle East. Among non-elites, the unemployment, housing and welfare problems faced by migrant workers in Europe contribute significantly to cultural and political marginalisation.[8]

The View from 'Muslim-majority' Countries

The first point to note here is that the term 'Muslim-majority' countries might have grouped together Bosnia, Turkey and Egypt, but the case studies reveal a variance that challenges this categorisation. Thus Bosnia in particular, being

---

[7]   On the remarkable similarities between policy and discourse on migrants described as 'Muslim' today, and (often the same) migrants described as 'Asians' or 'blacks' four decades ago, see Avtar Brah, *Cartographies of Diaspora, Contesting Identities* (London: Routledge, 1996) and Paul Gilroy, *There Ain't No Black in the Union Jack* (London: Routledge, 1995).

[8]   On race and class, see Gilroy, *Union Jack*, 1995.

both 'European' and home to a large 'Muslim' population, will be compared with the other two case studies here, but will be reconsidered alone in the next section. On the other hand, the three case studies do make one important empirical observation in common: there is a recurrent ambivalence in these countries' media representations of Europe. Europe's status hovers between two poles: at one end of the spectrum, it is rejected as coloniser, foreigner and infidel. At the other, it is welcomed as moderniser, as the desirable image of a better self, and a rationalising influence on religion. In Finkel and Sarajlić's analyses, Turkish and Bosnian Muslims mostly perceive Europe as a normative good and an eternal goal, but at times, they see it as deviating from that good, and thus as hypocritical in its dealings. This is reflected in fluctuating Turkish attitudes towards the European Union – sometimes indignant, sometimes deferent, always passionate – and in the diverse reactions to the Danish cartoon crisis among Muslim communities in different countries.

To conceptualise these differences, we might draw upon Finkel's idea of the different *sorts of battles* which the European Union and the three 'Muslim' case countries are fighting. To understand the conceptions of Europe in the latter, a simple analytical distinction can be made between the battles of the developed and developing worlds. While the European Union faces the challenges of building a multicultural yet supranational organisation, Bosnia, Turkey and Egypt are struggling – to different degrees of course – with issues of economic development, political sovereignty and autonomy. As we have seen, these are all necessarily managed in a dynamic with the EU that cannot escape certain historical legacies, most often of imperial threat or colonial conquest. Avenues for improving relations have emerged in recent decades, through EU accession processes and, in Egypt's case, the Euro-Mediterranean Partnership. Yet in each country, there are perceptions of continued economic or political dependency on Europe, which produce the ambiguous images of Europe we have seen in media and political discourses.

Thus in Egypt, the aftermath of decolonisation and the rise of the American superpower has, as Hanaa Ebeid explains, produced a Europe that can by turns be an ally, an aid donor and even a political model for Arab unity. In Turkey, the War of Independence was followed by the consolidation of Turkey's place within the NATO alliance. Yet an ambiguity persists, which sees Turkey and Egypt aspire to closer ties with Europe in their different ways, but remain preoccupied with autonomy in foreign affairs and threats to national unity. For many Turks, relations with Brussels can at times evoke the historical memory of nineteenth century European expansionism and the dismemberment of the Ottoman Empire after World War I. Meanwhile, many Egyptians see today's situation as reminiscent of old colonial dependency. This elicits a range of comparable reactions – from Turkish leaders trying to recast EU reforms as national policy, to both Turkish and Egyptian or Arab nationalists' outrage at overly interfering European prescriptions. In Pnina Werbner's words, 'todays architects of the New Europe confront the political fact that the past cannot be *made* to die...'[9] It is arguably at times when EU relations become strained – whether over EU accession or prescriptions for reform – that images of historical enmities are resurrected. These can be tapped by different political actors according to their various outlooks. Particularly in countries seeking EU membership, as Finkel writes of Turkey, Europe can become a 'cipher through which domestic wrangles and historic shifts in the balance of elite power are played out.' In Bosnia for example, the legacy of imperial and Cold War encounters with Western Europe was a construction of Europe and the Balkans as opposite poles in what Sarajlić calls a 'value order'. Yet, as he describes,

---

[9]   Pnina Werbner, 'Afterword: Writing Multiculturalism and Politics in the New Europe' in Werbner and Tariq Modood eds., *The Politics of Multiculturalism in the New Europe: Racism, Identity and Community* (London: Zed Books, 1997), p. 261.

recent Bosnian nation building projects have been funded and executed by EU agencies, and visibly emphasise the Europeanness of Bosnian identity.

Responding to these different histories of inter-state relations, the contributors to this volume have highlighted the interaction between events within and beyond the borders of their case countries. The authors of the 'Muslim-majority' case studies cite the historical reasons for the sensitivity in some Muslim societies to events of political import in European capitals or in the EU. Thus they have all examined international events, from the Iranian Revolution to the September 11th attacks, showing how they can transmit powerful currents that can be felt in 'local' politics far from their source. By the same token, events which began as 'domestic' in Europe have been shown to have loud echoes in distant locations. Ebeid provides examples such as the impact of Europe's handling of the Arab-Israeli conflict on conceptions of Europe among Egyptian media consumers. These dynamics, with the media as their vehicle, should be understood if popular reaction is not to be misrepresented through the narrow lens of religion or culture.

Indeed, conducting 'multilevel' analyses evidences once again the overdetermination of religion as an explanatory factor for popular political mobilisation. The impacts in Muslim-majority countries of the Danish cartoon crisis, or the Rushdie Affair before it, are cases in point. Firstly, both elicited a diverse set of reactions across the 'Islamic world', which, as James Piscatori points out, 'calls into question the gravity that can be attributed to the concept of an "Islamic issue"' in world politics.[10] Secondly, while ostensibly religiously motivated, some of these reactions can be more accurately understood within the context of grievances at structural imbalances of power vis-à-vis Europe and the United States, which culminated most recently in the wars on Afghanistan, Iraq, Lebanon and now Gaza. Considering that the 'war

---

[10] See James Piscatori, 'The Rushdie affair and the politics of ambiguity', *International Affairs*, Vol. 66, No. 4 (1990), p. 782.

on terror' has constructed a monolithic Islamic enemy, a religious self-identification in the ensuing backlash is unsurprising. This is compounded by perceptions of complicity on the part of governments in Muslim societies, and, in many cases, their authoritarian nature. In countries like Egypt, this 'puts a premium on such alternative outlets as the mosque or informal social gathering... "Islam" provides both the vocabulary and the outlet for the expression of oppositional sentiment.'[11] Yet the concerns that motivate these ostensibly religious or cultural protests can in fact be deeply secular in essence – they are connected far less with the spiritual or metaphysical and far more with political power relations between states or with concerns for material wellbeing among their populations.

The View from 'in between'

While this volume's 'European' and 'Muslim-majority' case studies have already exposed the inadequacy of cultural explanations for so-called 'Muslim politics',[12] this can be further demonstrated by offering one more case for consideration. The European/Muslim-majority dichotomy leaves one particular group unrepresented, even though much of the controversy described revolves around their situation: the Muslim communities of Europe. These are arguably the only group who identify most consistently, if at different times and in different locations, with either side of the purported 'European-Muslim' divide, and who are arguably sympathetic with, as well as squeezed by, trends in both. Exploring their example should serve to highlight the undue emphasis placed on the cultural (and religious) facets of what are often far more material, and always thoroughly political, struggles and aspirations among them.

---

[11] *Ibid.*, p. 773.
[12] For an anti-essentialist, insightful analysis, see Dale Eickelman and Piscatori, *Muslim Politics* (Princeton, New Jersey: Princeton University Press, 1996).

137

How do the themes traced throughout our 'European' and 'Muslim-majority' case studies resonate with the experience of these Muslims living in the heartlands of 'Christian' Europe? Debates among certain actors in the former two sets of case studies can be described as revolving around the questions of 'who speaks for Europe' and 'who speaks for Islam', respectively. In the case of 'European Muslims', both questions are asked at once, and this produces a unique set of debates that merit separate consideration. The first case to consider is that of Bosnia, particularly in terms of the interesting sub-phenomenon of Muslim migration to a Muslim society. Sarajlić describes a largely secular media that forge a 'media myth of Europe' which is characteristic of transition societies, and which posits a normatively superior Europe. He also describes a tension with Muslim leaders who champion their own conceptions of Islam in turn, and propose a political identity *as* Muslim in Bosnia, and in the EU framework. Here, Sarajlić's media analysis highlights the different dilemmas this political identity creates *among* Muslims, as such conceptions shut out the secular as well as the non-Muslims in Bosnian society, the migrants among whom may not so easily protest. In both cases, Bosniak actors wish to speak both for Europe and for Islam, and the media plays host to their competition.

A second case, and one which merits a future media analysis, is that of the Muslim immigrant (or second generation) communities in Europe. On the one hand, in some social and institutional contexts, they are confronted by evolving prejudices in their host countries, such as the thinly veiled Islamophobia of recent years. These are discourses that envelop and alienate even the most secular Muslims: they can push them to identify with even the most imagined or indeed imaginary of origins. This is compounded by a sensitivity to structures of dependency and exploitation between Europe and their countries of origin. The resulting alienation can generate a myriad of political outcomes, from apathy to radical action. These may well be communicated through a religious idiom drawn from political movements outside – and increasingly inside – Europe.

On the other hand, such individuals are often committed to survival in Europe, and therefore have an interest in integrating into their host society, both out of economic and psychological needs. Many lack the choice to 'go back' – whether due to political or economic pressures, or because they have never known their parents' homeland as their own. Indeed, many such migrants and their offspring subscribe sincerely to what they perceive as core values in Europe and the quality of life it offers, which they contrast with the heavy-handedness of the US or with the illiberal polities of their countries of origin. Their political choices thus often conform to the institutional traditions of their European context, whether in local or national politics.[13]

Between these two poles of identification and political action, then, is a wide spectrum in which Muslim communities in Europe might occupy different positions at different times, sometimes even at the same time, depending on the material and cultural matters at stake. In this sense, their experience can be understood by drawing upon the literature on diaspora:

> Diaspora refers to the doubled relationship of dual loyalty that migrants, exiles, and refugees have to places... Diasporic populations frequently occupy no singular cultural space but are enmeshed in circuits of social, economic, and cultural ties encompassing both the mother country and the country of settlement.[14]

Employing the diaspora paradigm here does not imply an acceptance of the racialisation of Muslims into one category, nor the view that Muslim immigrants will not integrate into their host societies. On the contrary, it is

---

[13] For a variety of case studies, see Ajaya Kumar Sahoo and Brij Maharaj eds., *Sociology of Diaspora: A Reader*, Vols. I and II (Jaipur and New Delhi: Rawat Publications, 2007).

[14] Smadar Lavie and Ted Swedenburg eds., *Displacement, Diaspora, and Geographies of Identity* (Durham and London: Duke University Press, 1996) p. 14.

very specifically used to foster an appreciation of the diversity of the cultural origins and choices of Muslim communities. While it allows for those who express their identities by reference to Islam, it also highlights the place of religion as just one among many identifiers in that array. Thus in many understudied cases, 'Living in the border is frequently to experience the feeling of being trapped in an impossible in-between, like cosmopolitan Franco-Maghrebis who are denied the option of identifying with either France or Algeria and are harassed both by white racist extremists and Islamist xenophobes.'[15] Once again, it is worth emphasising the material factors, such as class, education and employment opportunities, which impact upon migrants' cultural identifications. Samad, Deltombe and Hafez have all noted the very concrete structures and power imbalances that still do exist to divide and exclude along 'European/Muslim' lines, with all their sombre implications for the meanings of multiculturalism, (European) integration and postcoloniality today. Yet even in diaspora literature, there are fewer enquiries into the material circumstances of life as a migrant or refugee, while discourse analyses of its cultural – and religious – dimensions abound, often conducted in isolation from the former. Such accounts can display an ironic cultural insensitivity, as Terry Eagleton laments: 'If men and women need freedom and mobility, they also need a sense of tradition and belonging... The postmodern cult of the migrant, which sometimes succeeds in making migrants sound even more enviable than rock stars, is a good deal too supercilious in this respect.'[16]

The media as source

Media analysis has been a highly effective method in this volume's investigations – what role have the media been shown to play in political

---

[15]   Lavie and Swedenburg, *Displacement*, 1996, p. 15.
[16]   Eagleton, p. 21.

swings to the right, for example, and in their historical precedents? For political elites, the media provide perhaps the most powerful means by which to inscribe self/Other stereotypes in the public domain, as well as to legitimise policy. The case studies in this volume have illustrated the various ways in which journalists and news producers can be connected to political elites, whether through financial, familial or ideological ties. These can cause media outlets to mirror the government line on political issues quite closely, and particularly in times of heightened tension or officially declared national crisis. Tabloid-style distortion is arguably just as visible in broadsheet press at such times, and has been instrumental in concretising the phenomenon of moral panic.[17]

On the other hand, the prominent voices of dissent in British, French and German media have been acknowledged in the workshop and in this volume, and particularly by Kai Hafez. Thus while the contributors have highlighted the persistence of nationalist, exclusionist and at times, racist discourses in European politics, they have also noted the growth of public spaces for cultural expression on the part of minority communities in Europe. An important methodological point can be made here, relating specifically to media analysis. At times, it can bring out the worst in public debate, as a researcher may develop a selective bias when his/her topic is racism, for example. It is therefore important to be aware of competing arguments and to make use of a wide range of media sources. On the other hand, it is crucial to preserve a sense of the relative weight of such alternative discourses, and their political impact.[18] A focus on progressive but marginal discourses can distort the image ultimately presented of the media under scrutiny.

---

[17] See Rayen Salgado-Pottier, 'A modern moral panic: the representation of British Bangladeshi and Pakistani youth in relation to violence and religion', *Anthropology Matters*, Vol. 10, No. 1 (2008), p. 8.

[18] See Ronan Bennett, 'Shame on us', *The Guardian*, 19 November 2007.

***

This volume opened by seeking a way out of the literature's entrapment in the 'cultural fundamentalism' on both sides of the purported 'clash of civilisations'. This search continues to be a pressing one. Yet this volume's contributors have also described significant openings in debates on the future of integration and multiculturalism. In emphasising the dynamics between culture and class, past and present, national and international, this volume underlines the importance of widening our horizons when dealing with issues of similarly vast scope. Only with this sort of approach can we appreciate Islam's salience in political idioms across the globe with such different connotations, without misreading this as an irrational or uniform phenomenon. The next search should be for new analytical terms in which to comprehend these processes, and with which to transcend – at least in the scholarship – our 'mutual misunderstandings'.

Selected Bibliography

Alexander, Claire. 'Violence, Gender and Identity: Re-Imagining "The Asian Gang"' in Y. Samad and K. Sen eds., *Islam in the European Union: Transnationalism, Youth and the War on Terror* (Karachi: Oxford University Press, 2007).

Allen, Christopher and Jorgen S. Nielsen. *Summary Report on Islamophobia in the EU after 11 September 2001*, European Monitoring Centre on Racism and Xenophobia, Vienna, 2002.

Anderson, Benedict. *Imagined Communities: Reflections on the Origin and Spread of Nationalism* (London: Verso, 1991).

Arendt, Hannah. 'Truth and Politics', *The New Yorker*, 25 February 1967.

_____. 'Lying in Politics: Reflections on The Pentagon Papers', *The New York Review of Books*, 18 November 1971.

Bagguley, Paul and Yasmin Hussain. 'Conflict and cohesion: official constructions of "community" around the 2001 "riots" in Britain", *Critical Studies*, Vol. 28, 2006.

Bakic-Hayden, Milica. *Nesting Orientalisms: The Case of Former Yugoslavia*, *Slavic Review*, Vol. 54, No. 4, Winter 1995, pp. 917-931.

Barker, Martin. *The New Racism: Conservatives and the ideology of the tribe* (London: Junction Books, 1981).

Baubérot, Jean. *Laïcité 1905-2005, entre passion et raison* (Paris: Seuil, 2004).

Benson, Sue. 'Asians have Culture, West Indians have Problems: Discourses of Race and Ethnicity in and out of Anthropology', in T. Ranger et al., *Culture, Identity and Politics: Ethnic Minorities in Britain*, (Avebury: Aldershot, 1996).

Bigo, Didier. 'Identifier, catégoriser et contrôler. Police et logique proactive', in Laurent Bonelli and Gilles Sainati, *La Machine à punir* (Paris: L'Esprit frappeur, 2004).

Bouamama, Said. *L'Affaire du foulard Islamique. La production d'un racisme respectable* (Roubaix: Editions du Geai bleu, 2004).

Bougarel, Xavier. *The Role of Balkan Muslims in Building a European Islam,* European Policy Centre issue paper No. 43, 2005.

Bourdieu, Pierre. 'Un problème peut en cacher un autre', in Charlotte Nordmann ed., *Le foulard islamique en questions* (Paris: Amsterdam, 2004).

Brah, Avtar. *Cartographies of Diaspora, Contesting Identities* (London: Routledge, 1996).

Bringa, Tone. *Being Muslim the Bosnian Way: Identity and Community in a Central Bosnian Village* (Princeton: Princeton University Press, 1995).

Brossat, Alain. 'Europe: Us and Others' in *European Identity of Kosova,* International Symposium, Forum 2015, Pristina, 2008, pp. 25–31.

Brown, Demetra Vaka. *The Unveiled Ladies of Istanbul,* reprinted from the 1923 edition (New Jersey: Gorgias Press, 2005).

Cantle, Ted. *Community Cohesion: A New Framework for Race and Diversity* (Palgrave Macmillan, 2005).

Cassirer, Ernst. *Language and Myth* (New York and London: Harper & Bros., 1946).

Champagne, Patrick. 'La vision médiatique', in Pierre Bourdieu ed., *La Misère du monde* (Paris: Seuil, 1993).

Champagne, Patrick and Dominique Marchetti. *Censures visibles, censures invisibles* (Paris: Les Dossiers de l'audiovisuel, No. 106, INA, November 2002).

Cohen, Anthony P. *The Symbolic Construction of Community* (London: Tavistock, 1985).

Cohen, Stanley. *Folk Devils and Moral Panics* (London: Mac Gibbon and Kee, 1972).

Coles, Kimberly. 'Ambivalent Builders: Europeanization, the Production of

Difference and Internationals in Bosnia and Herzegovina', in Bougarel, X., E. Helms and G. Duijzings, eds., *The New Bosnian Mosaic: Identities, Memories and Moral Claims in a Post-War Society* (London: Ashgate, 2007).

Critcher, Chas. *Critical Readings: Moral Panics in the Media* (Berkshire: Open University Press, 2006).

Cusset, François. *La décennie. Le grand cauchemar des années 1980* (Paris: La Découverte, 2006).

Daniel, Jean. *Cet étranger qui me ressemble* (Paris: Grasset, 2004).

Deltombe, Thomas. 'Les médias français et les représentations du Prophète', contribution to the conference organised by the *Institut Français des Relations Internationales* (IFRI), 'Médias et construction des identités collectives en Méditerranée', Casablanca, November 2006.

Dietrich, Jung ed. *Democratization and Development: New Political Strategies for the Middle East*, (New York: Palgrave McMillan, Danish Institute for International Studies, 2006).

Drakulić, Slavenka. *Café Europa: Life After Communism* (Penguin, 1996).

Dröge, Franz W. *Publizistik und Vorurteil* (Münster: Regensberg, 1967).

Eagleton, Terry. *After Theory* (London: Penguin Books, 2004).

Ebeid, Hanaa. 'The Partnership in Southern Eyes: Reflections on the Discourse in the Egyptian Media', *EuroMeSCo papers*, issue no. 27, October 2004.

Eickelman, Dale and James Piscatori, *Muslim Politics* (Princeton, New Jersey: Princeton University Press, 1996).

Eribon, Didier. *D'une révolution conservatrice, et ses effets sur la gauche française* (Paris: Editions Leo Scheer, 2007).

Essam Eldin, Mohamed ed. *Media in the Arab World: Between Liberalisation and Reproducing Hegemony* (Cairo: Cairo Institute for Human Rights Studies, 2007). (Arabic).

Fraser, Nancy. *Transnationalizing the Public Sphere*, in Republicart, multilingual web journal, 2005.

Galtung, Johan and Mari Holmboe Ruge. 'The Structure of Foreign News', *Journal of Peace Research*, Vol. 2, No. 1, pp. 64-91.

Gastaut, Yvan. *L'immigration et l'opinion en France sous la Vie République* (Paris: Seuil, 2000).

Georges, Fawaz. *America and Political Islam: Clash of Cultures or Clash of Interests* (Cambridge: Cambridge University Press, 1999).

Gilroy, Paul. 'The End of Anti-Racism', *New Community*, 1990.

_____. *There Ain't No Black in the Union Jack* (London: Routledge, 1995).

Girardet, Raoul. *Politički mitovi i mitologije*, XX Vek, Beograd, 2000, [*Mythes et Mythologies Politiques*, Paris: Seuil, 1986].

Hafez, Kai. 'The Middle East and Islam in Western Media: Towards a Comprehensive Theory of Foreign Reporting', in Hafez ed., *Islam and the West in the Mass Media. Fragmented Images in a Globalizing World* (Cresskill, NJ: Hampton Press, 2000), pp. 27-66.

_____. *Die politische Dimension der Auslandsberichterstattung*, Vol.1: *Theoretische Grundlagen*, Vol. 2: *Das Nahost- und Islambild in der deutschen überregionalen Presse* (Baden-Baden: Nomos, 2002).

_____. 'Die irrationale Fehlwahrnehmung des "anderen": Deutsche und arabische Öffentlichkeitsreaktionen auf den 11. September', in Georg Stein and Volkhard Windfuhr eds., *Ein Tag im September 11.9.2001* (Heidelberg: Palmyra, 2002), pp. 221-246.

_____. 'The Iraq War 2003 in Western Media and Public Opinion. A Case Study of the Effects of Military (Non-) Involvement on Conflict Perception', *Global Media Journal*, Vol. 2, No. 5, 2004.

_____. *The Myth of Media Globalization* (Cambridge: Polity, 2007).

Halimi, Serge. *Les nouveaux chiens de garde* (Paris: Liber-Raison d'agir, 1997).

Hall, Stuart, et al. *Policing the Crisis: Mugging, the State and Law and Order* (London Macmillan Press, 1978).

Halliday, Fred. 'Islamophobia Reconsidered', *Ethnic and Racial Studies*, Vol. 22, No. 5, September 1999.

Heineman Jnr, Benjamin W. *The Politics of the Powerless: A Study of the Campaign Against Racial Discrimination* (London: Oxford University Press, 1972).

Herzfeld, Michael. *Cultural Intimacy: Social Poetics in the Nation-state* (London: Routledge, 2004), 2nd edition.

Hickman, Mary. 'The State, the Catholic Church and the Education of the Irish in Britain', in T. Ranger Y. Samad and O. Stuart eds., *Culture, Identity and Politics: Ethnic Minorities in Britain* (Aldershot: Avebury, 1996).

_____. '"Binary Opposites" or "Unique Neighbours"? The Irish in Multi-ethnic Britain', *Political Quarterly*, Vol. 71, No. 1, 2000.

Hiro, Dilip. *Black British, White British: A History of Race Relations in Britain* (London: Grafton Books, 1991).

Hobsbawm, Eric. *Nations and Nationalism since 1780: Programme, Myth, Reality* (Cambridge: Cambridge University Press, 1990).

Huntington, Samuel P. 'The Clash of Civilizations?', *Foreign Affairs*, Vol. 72, No. 3, 1993, pp. 22-49.

_____. *The Clash of Civilisations and the Remaking of World Order* (London: Touchstone Books, 1998).

Iskandar, Soheir, *The Egyptian Press and National Issues 1946-1954*, (Cairo: The Egyptian National Book Association, 1992).

Jeanneney, Jean-Noël, ed. *L'Echo du siècle. Dictionnaire historique de la radio et de la télévision en France* (Paris: Hachette Littérature/Arte Editions, 2001).

Kamrava, Mehran, ed. *The New Voices of Islam. Reforming Politics and Modernity. A Reader* (London et al: I.B. Tauris, 2006).

Karčić, Fikret. *Bosniaks and the Challenges of Modernity: the Late Ottoman and Habsburg Period* (Sarajevo: El-Kalem, 2004).

Kepel, Gilles. *Jihad: The Trail of Political Islam* (London: I.B. Tauris, 2002).

_____. *Les banlieues de l'Islam. Naissance d'une religion en France* (Paris: Seuil, 1987).

Khalid, Duran. *Re-Islamisierung und Entwicklungspolitik* (Munich et al: Weltforum Verlag, 1982).

Kuzma, Cindy. 'Rights and Liberties: Sex, Lies, and Moral Panics', *AlterNet*, 28 September 2005.

Kymlicka, Will. *Politics in the Vernacular: Nationalism, Multiculturalism and Citizenship* (Oxford: Oxford University Press, 2001).

Lavie, Smadar and Ted Swedenburg eds., *Displacement, Diaspora, and Geographies of Identity* (Durham and London: Duke University Press, 1996).

Lewis, Bernard. 'The Roots of Muslim Rage', *The Atlantic*, September 1990.

Lockman, Zachary. *Contending Visions of the Middle East. The History and Politics of Orientalism* (Cambridge: Cambridge University Press, 2004).

Mamdani, Mahmood. *Good Muslim, Bad Muslim: America, the Cold War, and the Roots of Terror* (Lahore: Vanguard Books, 2005).

Mbembe, Achille. 'La République et l'impensé de la race', in Nicolas Bancel, Pascal Blanchard and Sandrine Lemaire eds., *La Fracture coloniale* (Paris: La Découverte, 2005).

Menessy, Ahmed, ed. *The Media and Political Reform in Egypt*, (Cairo: Al-Ahram Centre for Political and Strategic Studies, 2007). (Arabic)

Mercier, Arnaud. *Le Journal télévisé* (Paris: Presses de Sciences-Po, 1996).

Mills-Affif, Edouard. *Filmer les immigrés* (Brussels: De Boeck, 2004).

Mitchell, Mark and D. Russell. 'Race, the New Right and State Policy', in T. Khushner and K. Lunn eds., *The Politics of Marginality: Race, the Radical Right and Minorities in Twentieth Century Britain* (London: Frank Cass, 1990).

Modood, Tariq. 'Political Blackness and British Asians', *Sociology*, Vol. 28, No.

4, 1994.

Moore, Barrington Jnr. *The Social Origins of Dictatorship and Democracy* (London: Allen Lane, 1967).

Morin, Edgar. *Penser L'Europe* (Gallimard: Paris, 1987)].

Morris, Chris. *The New Turkey: the quiet revolution on the edge of Europe* (London: Granta Books, 2005)

Mosses, George. *Toward the Final Solution* (Madison: University of Wisconsin, 1985).

Mueller, John E. *War, Presidents, and Public Opinion* (New York: Wiley, 1973).

Ousley, Herman. *Community Pride, Not Prejudice* (Bradford: Bradford Vision, 2001).

Öktem, Kerem. 'Being Muslim at the Margins: Alevis and the AKP', *Middle East Report*, No. 246, 2008.

Pamuk, Orhan. *Snow* (New York: Faber and Faber Limited, 2004).

Piscatori, James. 'The Rushdie affair and the politics of ambiguity', *International Affairs*, Vol. 66, No. 4 (1990).

Plenel, Edwy and Alain Rollat. *L'Effet Le Pen* (Paris: La Découverte - Le Monde, 1984).

Rimbert, Pierre. *Libération de Sartre à Rothschild* (Paris: Liber-Raison d'agir, 2005).

Roy, Olivier. *L'Islam mondialisé* (Paris: Seuil, 2002).

Rugh, William. *Arab Mass Media. Newspapers, Radio and Television in Arab Politics* (Westport and London: Praeger, 2004).

Runnymede Trust Commission on British Muslims and Islamophobia, *Islamophobia: a challenge for us all*, The Runnymede Trust, London, 1997.

Said, Edward. *Orientalism* (New York: Vintage Books, 1979).

_____. *Covering Islam. How the Media and the Experts Determine how We*

See the Rest of the World (New York: Pantheon Books, 1981).

Sahoo, Ajaya Kumar and Brij Maharaj eds. *Sociology of Diaspora: A Reader*, Vols. I and II (Jaipur and New Delhi: Rawat Publications, 2007).

Sakr, Naomi, ed. *Arab Media and Political Renewal: Community, Legitimacy and Public Life* (London: I.B. Tauris, 2007).

Rayen Salgado-Pottier. 'A modern moral panic: the representation of British Bangladeshi and Pakistani youth in relation to violence and religion', *Anthropology Matters*, Vol. 10, No. 1 (2008).

Samad, Yunas. 'Book Burning and Race Relations: Political Mobilization of Bradford Muslims', *New Community*, Vol. 18, No. 4, 1992. pp. 507-519.

Schulz, Winfried. *Die Konstruktion von Realität in den Nachrichtenmedien* (Freiburg: Alber, 1976).

Siddique, Mohammed. *Moral spotlight on Bradford* (Bradford: M. S. Press, 1993).

Sifaoui, Mohamed. *L'Affaire des caricatures. Dessins et manipulations* (Paris: Privé, 2006).

Siracusa, Jacques. *Le JT, machine à décrire. Sociologie du travail des reporters à la télévision* (Brussels: De Boeck, 2001).

Sivanandan, Ambalavaner. *Communities of Resistance* (London: Verso, 1990).

Solomos, John. *Black Youth, Racism and the State: the Politics of Ideology and Policy* (Cambridge: Cambridge University Press, 1988).

Smith, Anthony. *Nationalism and Modernism* (New York: Routledge, 1998).

Stora, Benjamin. *La Gangrène et l'Oubli. La mémoire de la guerre d'Algérie* (Paris: La Découverte, 1991).

Thofern, Detlef. *Darstellungen des Islams in DER SPIEGEL. Eine inhaltsanalytische Untersuchung über Themen und Bilder der Berichterstattung von 1950 bis 1989* (Hamburg: Dr. Kovac, 1998).

Todorova, Maria. *Imagining the Balkans* (New York: Oxford University Press, 1997).

Tumber, Howard and Jerry Palmer. *Media at War. The Iraq Crisis* (London et al: Sage, 2004).

Unland, Elmar. *Die Dritte-Welt-Berichterstattung der Frankfurter Rundschau von 1950 bis 1984. Eine statistische Längsschnittanalyse* (Münster: Lit, 1986).

Valentine, Simon. Background Paper for Muslims and Community Cohesion Project, COMPAS, Oxford, 2006.

Webster, Colin. 'The construction of British Asian criminality', *International Journal of the Sociology of Law*, Vol. 25, 1997.

Werbner, Pnina and Tariq Modood eds. *The Politics of Multiculturalism in the New Europe: Racism, Identity and Community* (London: Zed Books, 1997).

Wieviorka, Michel. *The Arena of Racism* (London: Sage, 1995).

Zubaida, Sami. *Islam, the People and the State* (London: Routledge, 1989).

Author Biographies

Editors

Kerem Öktem is Research Fellow for the study of Muslim communities in Europe at St Antony's College, Oxford. Having read Middle Eastern Studies at Oxford and completed his D. Phil. on Turkish nationalism in 2006, he has worked on transnational networks in South East Europe and Turkey, and more recently, on conflicts around Islam and nationalism in Europe. He is editor of the volume *In the Long Shadow of Europe: Greeks and Turks in the era of Postnationalism* (2009, together with Kalypso Nicolaidis and Othon Anastasakis) and has published articles, inter alia, in *Nations and Nationalism*, *Journal of South East European and Black Sea Studies*, *European Journal of Turkish Studies*. He is a regular contributor to the Middle East Report Online.

Reem Abou-El-Fadl is a DPhil candidate in Politics at the Department of Politics and International Relations and St Antony's College, Oxford University. She works on the relationship between foreign policy and nation building, exploring this through the case studies of Turkey and Egypt in the 1950s. In 2008, she co-convened a seminar series entitled *The United Arab Republic: New Historical Perspectives* at the Middle East Centre of Oxford University, revisiting Egypt's regional role as well as wider political developments in the Arab world during the Cold War. She is also interested in contemporary challenges of development and inequality facing the Arab region. In this context, she has participated in a project for the United Nations Development Programme on quality assurance improvement in Arab higher education.

Authors

Thomas Deltombe is an independent journalist working on Islam in France and on the history of colonialism. Graduate of the Institut d'études politiques in Paris, he published his leading study on media constructions of Islam and

Islamophobia in France in 2005 (*L'Islam imaginaire: La construction médiatique de l'islamophobie en France, 1975-2005*). Recently, he co-edited a volume called *Au nom du 11 septembre... Les démocraties à l'épreuve de l'antiterrorisme* (2008, with Didier Bigo and Laurent Bonelli). He is currently based in Lille, France.

Hanaa Ebeid is senior researcher at the International Relations Unit, Al Ahram Center for Political and Strategic Studies, part of the Al Ahram Foundation in Cairo, Egypt. She is also a PhD Candidate at the Faculty of Economics and Political Science, Cairo University. She has published extensively on relations between Egypt and the European Union, and especially on political reform in the Arab world.

Andrew Finkel is a journalist who has worked in Turkey since 1989 for a variety of print and broadcast media including *The Daily Telegraph*, *The Times*, *The Economist*, *Time*, and CNN. He has also contributed opinion pieces and features to a large variety of other publications including *The Washington Post*, *Cornucopia* magazine and most recently Le *Monde Diplomatique*. More unusually he has worked in the Turkish language press both in the newsroom and as a featured columnist (*Sabah* and *Milliyet*) and appears regularly on Turkish television. He has contributed to academic publications on issues of press integrity and continues to write a regular column for *Today's Zaman* newspaper in Istanbul as well as pursue his career as a freelance correspondent.

Kai Hafez is Professor of International and Comparative Communication Studies and chair of the Department of Media and Communication Studies at the University of Erfurt. Currently, he is guest professor at the Institute of Sociology in Bern, and has been a frequent academic political advisor to German governments. Hafez is on the editorial boards of several academic magazines (inter alia, *Arab Media & Society*, *Middle East Journal of Culture* and *Communication, Journal for International Communication*). Among his books published in English are: *Islam and the West in the Mass Media* (2000), *The Islamic World and the West* (2000), *Mass Media, Politics, and Society in the Middle East* (2001), *Media Ethics in the Dialogue of Cultures. Journalistic Self-Regulation in Europe, the Arab World, and Muslim Asia* (2003) and *The Myth of Media Globalization* (2007).

Eldar Sarajlić received his Masters in Political Science from the Faculty of Political Science in Sarajevo. He has published articles and essays in various journals and periodicals in Bosnia and Herzegovina. He is affiliated with the Institute for Social Research at the Faculty of Political Science in Sarajevo, where he participates in a comprehensive research project on Bosnian political elites. Eldar also acts as an editor in the journals *Pulse of Democracy* and *Status* (www.pulsdemokratije.ba; www.status.ba) in Bosnia and Herzegovina. Currently, he works for the United Nations Development Programme office in Sarajevo as a Communications Associate.

UNIVERSITY OF
OXFORD

St Antony's
College
European Studies Centre